SAVING THE EUROPEAN UNION

SAVING THE EUROPEAN UNION

the Logic of the Lisbon Treaty

Andrew Duff

shoehorn

Shoehorn Current Affairs & History Books

First published in 2009 by

Shoehorn Media Ltd
4 Great Marlborough Street
London W1F 7HH
England

www.shoehorn.biz
www.shoehornbooks.com

Copyright © Andrew Duff

A CIP catalogue record for this book is available from the British Library.

ISBN: 978 1 907149 02 3

Printed in the UK by LSUK, Milton Keynes.

Cover photograph:
Gordon Brown, UK Prime Minister, signing the Treaty of Lisbon
and, from left to right, European Commission President José Manuel
Barroso, Portuguese Prime Minister José Socrates and
European Parliament President Hans-Gert Poettering.
Photograph courtesy of The Council of the European Union.

CONTENTS

In memory of Bronislaw Geremek

1932-2008

PREFACE

European Union treaties are quite complicated. They are also terribly important, especially for a European Union legislator, to understand, explain and try to justify. I have found, over the years, that the best way to comprehend and communicate an EU treaty is to write a book about it.

This book picks up the story of the Union's long and complex constitutional processes after the French and Dutch voters rejected the EU's 'constitutional treaty' in 2005. Of necessity, it draws on my previous publications, notably *The Struggle for Europe's Constitution* (Federal Trust & I.B. Tauris, 2005), *Plan B: How to Rescue the European Constitution* (Notre Europe, 2006), and *'Constitution Plus' renegotiating the treaty* (TEPSA, 2007). I am grateful to those publishers for giving me a test-bed, and to FT.com for letting me publish regular articles over these years as the Union has lurched from one constitutional episode to the next.

Many people in the EU institutions and in their orbit have wittingly and unwittingly encouraged me to write this book. Brussels is a very fertile place. Several of my parliamentary colleagues are a rich source of ideas and argumentation. In particular I have appreciated the contribution of my two MEP colleagues in the Lisbon IGC, Elmar Brok and Enrique Barón Crespo, as well as of the leading lights of the Parliament's Constitutional Affairs Committee: Richard Corbett, Sylvia Kaufmann, Jo Leinen, Inigo Méndez de Vigo and Johannes Voggenhuber. We deputies are well served by a number of dedicated officials of the Parliament. I have appreciated at close quarters the contribution of members and officials of the Barroso Commission. The constitutional picture is incomplete without acknowledgment of the work of the ministers and officials of the successive presidencies of the Council, and its permanent secretariat.

Outside the institutions, a number of free-lance thinkers have been especially stimulating about the Lisbon experience: David Coombes, Pat Cox, Peter Ludlow, Paolo Ponzano, Alastair Sutton – as well as several Brussels based journalists whom I will not disconcert by naming. I get good critical advice from colleagues in the European Council on Foreign Relations (ECFR), the Trans-European Policy Studies Association (TEPSA) and the Union of European Federalists (UEF). My party, the UK Liberal Democrats, and group, the Alliance for Liberals and Democrats for Europe (ALDE), have been amazingly tolerant of finding a militant federalist in their midst.

Lastly my assistants during this time have their fingerprints on the book: Roland Fleig, Tim Huggan, Joost Koomen, Sietse Wijnsma. Guillaume McLaughlin, my chief policy advisor, bears the brunt.

Andrew Duff
Brussels and Cambridge
February 2009

CHAPTER ONE   EUROPE AT RISK

On 7 May 1948, only three years after the end of the war in Europe, Winston Churchill presided over a 'Congress of Europe' in The Hague. This amazing gathering of Europe's democratic politicians included both former and future government leaders, such as Léon Blum, Paul Reynaud, Konrad Adenauer, François Mitterrand, Paul-Henri Spaak and Alcide De Gasperi, as well as influential federalists such as Jean Monnet, Salvador de Madriaga and the future first President of the European Commission, Walter Hallstein. The Congress was a remarkable feat of organisation. Even travelling to Holland was arduous in those days, with frequent delays and long stops at borders controlled by military police.

Sadly, these were mostly West European politicians. Mr Churchill's 'Iron Curtain' was already descending from Stettin in the Baltic to Trieste in the Adriatic.[1] The Communist coup d'état had just taken place in Czechoslovakia. The Russians were taking their first steps to blockade East Germany. The prospects for liberal democracy had already been suffocated in Poland.

Although many of the organisers of the Congress were British, the Labour government of the day, in the words of Roy Jenkins, displayed a 'reluctant tolerance of what they chose to regard as a rather frivolous event'.[2] Winston Churchill was not dismayed. He told the Congress:

---

[1] Churchill's Iron Curtain speech was delivered in Fulton, Missouri as early as March 1946. In September 1946, he had spoken in Zurich of the urgency of building 'a kind of United States of Europe'.

[2] Roy Jenkins, *Churchill*, 2001, p. 815.

'We must proclaim the mission and design of a United Europe whose moral conception will win the respect and gratitude of mankind, and whose physical strength will be such that none will dare molest her tranquil sway ... I hope to see a Europe where men and women of every country will think of being European as of belonging to their native land, and wherever they go in this wide domain will truly feel 'Here I am at home'.'

After five days and nights of hard work, the Congress ended with a declaration which managed to combine inspiration with practical proposals. The statement is the founding document of the international European Movement, and led indirectly to the establishment of the Council of Europe in 1949 (this time with the British and Irish) and, one year later, to the launching of the European Coal and Steel Community (again without the British or Irish) by Jean Monnet and Robert Schuman.

The 1948 'Message to Europeans' still has the power to move:

MESSAGE TO EUROPEANS

Europe is threatened, Europe is divided, and the greatest danger comes from her divisions.

Impoverished, over laden with barriers that prevent the circulation of her goods but are no longer able to afford her protection, our disunited Europe marches towards her end. Alone, no one of our countries can hope seriously to defend its independence. Alone, no one of our countries can solve the economic problems of today. Without a freely agreed union our present anarchy will expose us tomorrow to forcible unification whether by the intervention of a foreign empire or usurpation by a political party.

The hour has come to take action commensurate with the danger.

Together with the overseas peoples associated with our destinies, we can tomorrow build the greatest political formation and the greatest economic unit our age has seen. Never will the history of the world have known so powerful a gathering of free men. Never will war, fear and misery have been checked by a more formidable foe.

Between this great peril and this great hope, Europe's mission is clear. It is to join her peoples in accordance with their genius of diversity and with the conditions of modern community life, and so open the way towards organised freedom for which the world is seeking. It is to revive her inventive powers for the greater protection and respect of the rights and duties of the individual of which, in spite of all her mistakes, Europe is still the greatest exponent.

Human dignity is Europe's finest achievement, freedom her true strength. Both are at stake in our struggle. The union of our continent is now needed not only for the salvation of the liberties we have won, but also for the extension of their benefits to all mankind.

Upon this union depend Europe's destiny and the world's peace.

Let all therefore take note that we Europeans, assembled to express the will of all the peoples of Europe, solemnly declare our common aims in the following five articles, which summarise the resolutions adopted by the Congress:

PLEDGE

1) We desire a United Europe, throughout whose area the free movement of persons, ideas and goods is restored;

2) We desire a Charter of Human Rights guaranteeing liberty of thought, assembly and expression as well as the right to form a political opposition;

3) We desire a Court of Justice with adequate sanctions for the implementation of this Charter;

4) We desire a European Assembly where the live forces of all our nations shall be represented;

5) And pledge ourselves in our homes and in public, in our political and religious life, in our professional and trade union circles, to give our fullest support to all persons and governments working for this lofty cause, which offers the last chance of peace and the one promise of a great future for this generation and those that will succeed it.

Much is said about the founding fathers of the United States of America. More needs to be known about the remarkable people who, in difficult times, laid the foundations of the European Union. In 1948 Europe found itself in great peril, yet it rescued itself with great hope and determination. Sixty years on, our dangers and challenges are somewhat different, but most of the same prescriptions apply. Whatever the European Union does today, it should be encouraged by its history. Human rights are respected and promoted. The Berlin Wall was pulled down twenty years ago. Most of Europe is re-united around the values of liberal democracy. The sovereignty of Europe's nation states is no longer under armed attack but is pooled willingly by democratic means in a federal union of interdependent states and a common citizenship. Europe's social welfare is vastly improved as we enjoy free movement of people, capital and goods within one single market. Sixteen states share the single currency of the euro, now ten years old. We have written a Charter of Fundamental Rights and created a European Court of Justice with an impressive corpus of supranational law. The European Parliament will be directly elected for the seventh time in 2009. Membership of the Union has grown from the original six countries in 1951 to twenty seven in 2007, with a population of 490 million.

The peril and the hope

The European Union has a good record of action: it must now promise more. Present conditions are still perilous. The global banking system has failed. It is clear that the current recession is the worst for fifty years, but we do not know its depth or its length. Meanwhile, the risk of protectionism returns. Russia is once again asserting itself, and is in a powerful position not least because it controls most of the EU's energy supply. Climate change threatens Europe's agriculture and sea levels in the short term – and in the long term catastrophe. Islamist fundamentalism poses challenges to the EU's internal security. The EU does not have the power to pacify the Middle East, and its interests are directly jeopardised by political instability in the large arc from Turkey to India. In Africa, poverty, disease and ethnic conflicts have impeded the hoped for progress.

Europeans have learned the hard way that they will be stronger together or weaker apart. How the EU emerges from its numerous present difficulties depends to a great extent on whether it can successfully strengthen its system of governance. Like the Americans before us, we face the classical liberal dilemma about what size of central government is necessary to deliver decent common solutions to our grave shared problems. After independence in 1776, the Americans discovered that a weak coalition of small states was not fit for purpose. Since 1945 Europeans have been undertaking a vast constitutional experiment in integration of which Mr Churchill's Congress in The Hague was instrumental. Treaties have come and gone, each building on the successes of the other, as well as learning from mistakes. Popular support for this federal process has at best been patchy and rarely solid. Old habits die hard: nationalism has a long history in Europe. The latest attempt to take a very important qualitative step forward towards a more federal union is the Treaty of Lisbon. It is the logical step for Europe to take.

CHAPTER TWO   WHAT THE TREATY SAYS

On 13 December 2007, at the magnificent Jeronimos monastery in Lisbon where Vasco da Gama is buried, a treaty was signed. Although British prime minister Gordon Brown was clumsily late for the ceremony, all heads of government of the twenty-seven member states of the European Union put their signatures to the new treaty.

The Treaty of Lisbon, if it enters into force, will transform the Union's system of governance and Europe's place in world affairs.

The Treaty of Lisbon substantially amends the *Treaty on European Union (TEU)* (essentially the Treaty of Maastricht of 1992) and the *Treaty establishing the European Community (TEC)* (essentially the Treaty of Rome of 1957). The latter is renamed the *Treaty on the Functioning of the European Union (TFEU)*. Both treaties, the TEU and TFEU, have the same legal rank.[3]

The Lisbon treaty was meant to come into force on 1 January 2009, but it did not.[4] Its delay – and possible annulment – is the latest twist in a long and complicated story. The Lisbon treaty was born in controversial circumstances after two previous draft treaties of the European Union had to be discarded.

The first of those failures was the product of a historic Convention on the Future of Europe which worked under the presidency of Valéry Giscard d'Estaing from February 2002 to July 2003. The Convention, which worked by consensus, was made up of representatives of the heads of government, the European Commission, national MPs and

---

[3] Article 1 TEU. The numbering of articles cited here is taken from the consolidated versions of the TEU and TFEU as they will be once Lisbon enters into force. OJ C 115, 09-05-2008.

[4] Article 6(2) Reform Treaty. OJ C 306, 17-12-2007.

Members of the European Parliament. The title of the Convention's product was *Draft Treaty establishing a Constitution for Europe*.[5] Once the heads of government had received this document, they handed it over to the clutches of a classical Intergovernmental Conference (IGC) made up of national diplomats and lawyers. The IGC laboured long and hard until unanimous agreement was reached on the *Treaty establishing a Constitution of Europe*, which was signed in Rome on 29 October 2004.[6]

Despite some watering down of certain provisions of the Convention's draft, this 2004 treaty was highly ambitious. It was still a constitutive treaty which re-cast the values and principles which lie behind European unification, consolidated the competences conferred on the Union by its member states, clarified the powers of the EU institutions, rationalised instruments, streamlined decision-making procedures and codified jurisprudence. What had previously been long-winded and obscure was now shortened and simplified. Certain ambiguities and inconsistencies thrown up by previous treaty revisions – Maastricht (1992), Amsterdam (1997) and Nice (2001) – were now resolved. The overall effect of the 2004 reform was to turn the pile of international treaties which has hitherto formed the basic statutes of the EU into a more visible and distinct supranational legal order.

A precursor of the Giscard Convention had been the Convention of 1999-2000 which drew up the Charter of Fundamental Rights. The constitutional treaty of 2004 made the Charter binding on the EU, bestowed on the Union a legal personality in terms of international law, and gave to the European Parliament the power to initiate future treaty amendment. These are three examples of what was properly described as a process of constitutionalisation. The effect of the 2004 treaty would have been to replace the Union's earlier treaties, and to re-found the Union on a more secure and constitutional basis.

---

[5] CONV 850/03, 18 July 2003
[6] OJ C 310, 16-12-2004.

The 2004 treaty, which was supposed to enter into force in November 2006, was never ratified. In May and June 2005 referendums in France and the Netherlands rejected the constitutional treaty, in part because of its overt constitutional nature. A long period of reflection followed until the then German presidency of the European Council brokered a deal. In March 2007 a Berlin Declaration, marking the fiftieth anniversary of the Treaty of Rome, promised that the Union would be advancing again on a 'renewed common basis' by 2009.[7] In July, under the Portuguese presidency, a new IGC was quickly set to work, and the result was the Treaty of Lisbon.

The effect of Lisbon was to further modify the package that had been agreed by the constitutional Convention. To placate the French and Dutch some of the more overtly constitutional elements, such as the Charter, the flag and anthem, were dropped from the text. The title of 'Foreign Minister' was changed back into 'High Representative'. Instead of replacing the earlier treaties, Lisbon merely sought to amend them heavily. Protocols with complicated opt-outs from key areas of common policy were added for the benefit of Denmark, Ireland the United Kingdom, the three (somewhat troublesome) countries that had joined the European Community late, in 1973.

Some of the clarity gained in the earlier formulations was sacrificed: for example, the nomenclature of European 'laws' in the constitutional treaty was changed back into the old 'regulations' and 'directives'. In some ways, the Lisbon exercise was merely an obscurantist one, undertaken deliberately to allow France, the Netherlands and the UK to escape from their previous hubristic pledges to hold referendums. But the basic reforms survived. The Charter of Fundamental Rights, although excised from the treaty itself, was given the full force of primary law of the Union. The blue flag with the twelve gold stars and Beethoven's Ode to

---

[7] Berlin Declaration,
http://europa.eu/50/docs/berlin_declaration_en.pdf

Joy are still to be used to symbolise the Union. And the High Representative keeps all the powers and responsibilities of the soi-disant Foreign Minister.[8]

The original intention to achieve transparency and simplicity was not respected. Not only are we left with two treaties rather than one, but also with two annexes, thirty-seven protocols and sixty-five declarations.

Despite setbacks on the way, the Treaty of Lisbon still represents a historic step forward for European unification at least on a par with the Treaty of Maastricht which established the constitutional concept of EU citizenship, introduced the single currency and expanded EU competence into the field of foreign and security policy. And Maastricht had signatories from only twelve countries; Lisbon has twenty seven, representing nearly 500 million people.

As we know, the hoped for smooth ratification of the Lisbon treaty was interrupted by the Irish referendum in June 2008. Yet ratification has proceeded as intended in most of the other member states by parliamentary processes: at the time of writing only the parliament of the Czech Republic has to conclude its vote on Lisbon. And Ireland has agreed to have a second referendum on Lisbon in 2009, just as it had to on the Treaty of Nice in 2002. Europe still hopes for the Lisbon treaty. In the meantime it has to live and work on the basis of Nice, which was devised in fairly unfortunate circumstances by only fifteen of the present twenty-seven member states as long ago as December 2000.

If constitutional reform of the European Union is so difficult, why do we bother? The answer can lie only in a fairly detailed investigation of how Lisbon improves upon Nice.

---

[8] In fact only five articles of the 2004 constitutional treaty do not find their way somehow into Lisbon: Articles I-6 on the primacy of EU law (although this is replicated in a declaration to Lisbon), I-8 on the symbols, I-42 on the area of freedom, security and justice, IV-437 on the repeal of the earlier treaties, and IV-439 on transition arrangements.

The new treaty will much enhance the Union's capacity to act by increasing the efficiency and effectiveness of the institutions and decision-making mechanisms. Armed with the treaty, the EU will be able to face its new global challenges and address the issues which matter most to citizens – such as climate change, energy security, international terrorism, cross-border crime, asylum and immigration.

The Treaty of Lisbon will greatly improve the democratic character of the Union by increasing Parliament's powers, by entrenching the Charter of Fundamental Rights and by strengthening the rule of law. It clarifies the values and reaffirms the objectives of the Union.

Values, principles and objectives

The debate about the values and principles which guide the Union was far from academic, because it is these which, if breached, can provoke the suspension of a member state from the Union. Hierarchy matters in a constitutional legal order, and, besides, it was genuinely difficult for the treaty drafters to reflect in constitutional language the diversity of contemporary European society.[9]

No less difficult was the formulation of the catalogue of Union objectives.[10] Here, more starkly than with values, partisan preferences between left and right were in evidence. Having been patched together fairly unsystematically, the existing treaties offer no more than a jumbled check list of competing objectives. The new treaty succeeds in rationalising as well as modernising the provisions about what it is that the Union seeks to achieve, and writes them down in a clear and relatively succinct fashion, as follows:

ARTICLE 3, TREATY ON EUROPEAN UNION

1) The Union's aim is to promote peace, its values and the well-being of its peoples.

---

[9] Article 2 TEU.
[10] Article 3 TEU.

2) The Union shall offer its citizens an area of freedom, security and justice without internal frontiers, in which the free movement of persons is ensured in conjunction with appropriate measures with respect to external border controls, asylum, immigration and the prevention and combating of crime.

3) The Union shall establish an internal market. It shall work for the sustainable development of Europe based on balanced economic growth and price stability, a highly competitive social market economy, aiming at full employment and social progress, and a high level of protection and improvement of the quality of the environment. It shall promote scientific and technological advance.

It shall combat social exclusion and discrimination, and shall promote social justice and protection, equality between women and men, solidarity between generations and protection of the rights of the child.

It shall promote economic, social and territorial cohesion, and solidarity among Member States.

It shall respect its rich cultural and linguistic diversity, and shall ensure that Europe's cultural heritage is safeguarded and enhanced.

4) The Union shall establish an economic and monetary union whose currency is the euro.

5) In its relations with the wider world, the Union shall uphold and promote its values and interests and contribute to the protection of its citizens. It shall contribute to peace, security, the sustainable development of the Earth, solidarity and mutual respect among peoples, free and fair trade, eradication of poverty and the protection of human rights, in particular the rights of the

child, as well as to the strict observance and the development of international law, including respect for the principles of the United Nations Charter.

6) The Union shall pursue its objectives by appropriate means commensurate with the competences which are conferred upon it in the Treaties.

Again, hierarchy is important. The promotion of peace appears as the primordial objective of the Union, rather than as a value, which suggests that the EU is not a pacifist organisation. In the external field, moreover, the EU must work not only to observe international law, but to develop it.

Lisbon reaffirms some cardinal principles that have gradually shaped the Union's system of governance. Those include the basic freedoms of movement of people, goods, services and money on which the single market is built. These four freedoms are not just to be respected, but guaranteed by the Union. Another key principle of the Union outlaws discrimination on the grounds of nationality.[11]

As a direct counter-balance to the requirement for member states to obey the EU regime of the single market and non-discrimination on the grounds of nationality, an article is then inserted to establish states' rights. The Union explicitly recognises that it must not intrude into the national 'no go' areas, the 'essential state functions' concerning security, law and order and territorial integrity. The treaty breaks new ground by insisting that the EU institutions must respect the domestic constitutional structures of the states – including their variable systems of regional and local self-government.[12]

Previous EU treaties had restrained member states from impeding the successful accomplishment of the Union's

---

[11] Article 18 TFEU.
[12] Article 4(2) TEU.

objectives and had enjoined them to show mutual solidarity. In response to case law, a more concise articulation is now made of the need for states to help each other meet the demands and obligations of Union membership. The need for 'sincere co-operation' among member states on the one hand, and between them and the Union on the other, becomes a guiding principle of the new treaty. The states thereby recognise explicitly their mutual duty towards each other.[13]

The legal order

A key element in the relationship between the European Union and its states is the principle of the primacy – note, not the supremacy – of Union law. The principle has been established by jurisprudence of the Court of Justice from the earliest years.

What is meant by the primacy of EU law? The principle was most clearly established in an early judgment of the European Court of Justice. In Costa v. ENEL (1964) the Court found that, in contrast to ordinary international treaties, the European Community created its own legal system which became an integral and binding part of the national legal systems of member states.[14] EU law is directly applicable within member states. It is interpreted uniformly across the whole of the Union. It has direct effect, which means that it is applicable directly by national courts. EU law confers rights and obligations on citizens which national jurisdictions must seek to uphold. The states must ensure adequate remedies for breaches of EU law. Lisbon increases the powers of the Court and the Commission to impose penalties in case of infringement.[15]

---

[13] Article 4(3) TEU.
[14] Case 6/64 *Costa v. ENEL*, ECR 585. Subsequent jurisprudence has upheld and reinforced the precedence of EU law, notably *Internationale Handelsgesellschaft* (1970), *Simmenthal* (1978), *Factortame* (1990) and *Francovich* (1991).
[15] Article 260(2-3) TFEU.

Extensive use has been made of the facility by which national judges can refer to the Court of Justice for a preliminary ruling on questions of EU law. Accession to the Union means that a state accepts not only all current EU law but also all future EU law. National parliaments may not legislate to cause conflicts, intentional or not, with EU law. States are liable for breaches of EU law within their own national jurisdictions. It is the job of the European Court of Justice, seated at Luxembourg, to see that the law of the Union is observed and to rule on incompatibilities between EU and national law.

National courts have grown to be fairly receptive to the precedence they must give to EU law. Although the concept of EU supremacy over national constitutions has not been universally acknowledged by rulings of the constitutional courts of every state, national jurisdictions have been careful to avoid confrontation on this issue with the Court of Justice. Different states have adapted their own constitutions to reflect these realities in a number of ways. Dutch basic law is very precise about the precedence that must be given to the EU legal order; the German and Italian constitutions, by contrast, are rather vague on the matter. The relevant UK statute is the 1972 European Communities Act which gives legal effect to EU law.

To summarise, primacy of EU law means that wherever there is a conflict between an EU and a national law, it is the EU law that prevails to the extent necessary and the national law shall not apply. The implications for foreign, security and defence dimension of the EU are less far-reaching partly because there is no relevant EU legislation but also because the treaty deliberately limits the involvement of the Court of Justice in this area. One may live to regret this restricted role for the Court, however, if the states were to try to shelter from judicial review for their actions in foreign affairs behind the anonymity of the Union.

In any case, after much debate, the Treaty of Lisbon re-stated the principle of the primacy of EU law in a declaration.[16] In the 2004 constitutional treaty the concept of primacy had been accorded an article of its own. The change was made in response to President Sarkozy's demands that the constitutional character of the reform package should be downgraded. The French government was supported by the British and the Dutch; and the Germans conceded.

It follows from the fact that the Union enjoys an autonomous legal order that it is an entity to be acknowledged in its own right on the international stage. The Lisbon treaty acquires for the Union a single legal personality in international law across its whole competence.[17] Under the current and previous treaties, only the European Communities have enjoyed a *persona* in international law. The main effect of this change is to widen the scope of the powers of the European Commission to negotiate and sign treaties on behalf of the Union as a whole, including international conventions on the environment and aspects of external and internal security policy. The EU will be able to join international organisations in its own right, aiding both legal certainty and political transparency. Accordingly, the states may only sign international agreements that are compatible with EU law. Parliament has to approve all agreements in fields covered by the ordinary legislative procedure, association agreements, and those with budgetary or institutional implications. Exercised well, the Union's legal personality would enable it to become a more coherent global player in the context of the United Nations. It does not mean that the UK and France will have to give up their permanent seats on the UN Security Council. But it does mean that it will be easier for them to act as a single entity on behalf of the EU in circumstances where they and other EU states can agree on common positions.

One of the first practical results of the acquisition of legal personality will be an EU application to accede to the

---

[16] Declaration 17.
[17] Article 47 TEU.

1950 European Convention for the Protection of Human Rights and Fundamental Freedoms (ECHR).

The Charter of Fundamental Rights

Citizenship of the European Union was formally created by the Treaty of Maastricht (1992), largely at German and Spanish insistence, in order to give practical expression to the right of the individual to move freely around the single market. Practical benefits of EU citizenship were limited at first to an extension of the franchise for local authority and European Parliamentary elections in member states other than one's own, and to a widening of mutual diplomatic protection. The right to petition the Parliament as well as to approach the Parliamentary Ombudsman in cases of maladministration by one of the EU institutions were also introduced. Citizenship began to acquire more salience once the Treaty of Amsterdam (1997) expanded the Union's ambitions in the field of internal security policy. Amsterdam also installed an important extension to the competence of the EU, enabling it to 'combat discrimination based on sex, racial or ethnic origin, religion or belief, disability, age or sexual orientation'.[18]

Concerns that the fast pace of European integration was running too far ahead of the languid emergence of EU citizenship prompted the powerful German Constitutional Court in Karlsruhe to warn against any further transfer of competence in this field to the EU level without a concomitant strengthening of fundamental rights protection. The German government used its term of office as president of the Council in 1999 to propose the setting up of an EU-wide Convention to draft a Charter of Fundamental Rights.

The sixty-two strong Convention, made up of representatives of the heads of government, the Commission, and MEPs as well as national MPs, set to work. It succeeded, beyond the expectations of many, to draft by consensus. The result was a modern catalogue of the classical fundamental

---

[18] Article 13 TEC (now Article 19 TFEU).

rights as well as the principles which have guided the development of EU law and policy over the years. Its express purpose was to protect the citizen from any abuse by the EU of the power it exercises. The draft Charter of Fundamental Rights of the European Union, agreed on 2 October 2000, comprised fifty substantive articles, divided into chapters on dignity, freedoms, equality, solidarity, citizens' rights and justice. These were followed by four horizontal articles that set out the scope of the Charter, the limitations and level of protection of the rights, and prohibition of their abuse.

During the drafting of the Charter, particular controversies arose over the 'post-modern' provisions, such as eugenics and human cloning. Most difficult of all were the rights in the field of social policy, where the Charter had to avoid giving the impression that anyone without a job or a house could obtain one or the other merely by application to the EU courts.

In general, the self-image of European society formulated in the Charter is one of liberty and pluralism. Restrictions on freedom, for example in the area of data protection, have to be prescribed by laws that are to be enforced by an independent authority. Freedom of thought, conscience and religion is emphasised, as is the right to free expression. Frequent reference is made to the principle of subsidiarity, and the need for the EU institutions to respect national laws and practices. Throughout the Charter it is the right of the individual person that is articulated. The onus falls on each individual to respect the rights of others. Collective rights as such are eschewed in order to avoid treading upon the collective rights of other groups.

In December 2000 at Nice, the Charter was 'solemnly proclaimed' by the Council, Commission and Parliament. The IGC that was about to conclude the drafting of the Treaty of Nice declined to make the Charter justiciable in the courts, despite the fact that the Convention had drafted the Charter so that it could become mandatory. The Charter's focus was deliberately limited to the European Union institutions and agencies, at home and abroad, including member state governments when and in so far as they carry out EU law and policy. But desperate to avoid creating new legal obligations at European level, and fearful of nationalist reaction back home, the United Kingdom and Ireland continued to insist that the Charter should be treated merely as a political code of conduct.

Elsewhere, however, it was accepted that respect for fundamental rights requires not only parliamentary and judicial legitimacy but also wide social consensus. In any case, the Charter's social provisions are cast more as principles to guide the good government of the Union rather than as fundamental rights that can be guaranteed by way of a remedy delivered by the EU institutions. The result is that within the Charter some clauses enjoy more judicial automaticity than others. Clarity as to which is which became an obsession of the British government. Yet the Charter's status as a proclamation was ambiguous in terms of EU law, and actually served to invoke the very legal confusion that the British government was so anxious to avoid. Despite the fact that the UK government insisted that the Charter created no new legal obligations, the European Commission and European Parliament both undertook to be bound by its provisions, and the Court of Justice began to refer to the Charter in its case-law.

Eventually, under intense pressure from the Giscard Convention, the UK conceded that the Charter would become binding. Yet at the same time the British mounted a rearguard action to try to dilute the Charter's legal force. The horizontal clauses were adjusted in the 2004 constitutional treaty to make clearer the difference between classic rights (for a breach of which the courts have to seek direct remedies) and fundamental principles (which inform the formulation, enactment and implementation of EU law). However, even the UK accepted that complete separation between the two would be against the whole spirit of the Charter which aims to be a single and comprehensive catalogue of modern rights: and it was obvious that some provisions – such as those on gender equality – defy strict categorisation.[19]

The 2004 IGC added a clause to the Charter to say that the courts should give 'due regard' to the explanatory memorandum drawn up by the Praesidium of the Charter Convention.[20] These explanations are not in themselves justiciable, and would have been one tool of interpretation used by the courts in any case, regardless of where and how they were published. Of academic interest, the explanations describe the sources of each provision of the Charter in terms of the EU treaties, court jurisprudence, general principles of EU law and specific EU legislation, as well as relevant statutes of international law.

The Charter formed Part Two of the 2004 constitutional treaty. In the aftermath of the French and Dutch referendums, as part of the effort to reduce the constitutional character of the treaty, the Charter was removed. Nevertheless, under Lisbon the Charter is still made binding and has the same legal value as the treaties, although its text will not be in the treaty.[21] On 12 December 2007 the revised Charter was again solemnly proclaimed at a plenary session of the Parliament by the Presidents of the Parliament, the Council and the Commission and published in the *Official Journal*.[22]

A protocol to Lisbon introduces specific measures for the United Kingdom and Poland seeking to establish national exceptions to the justiciability of the Charter.[23] Apparently this retreat from 2004 was considered necessary to beguile

---

[19] Charter Articles 21 and 23; OJ C 303, 14-12-2007.

[20] Charter Article 52(7).

[21] Article 6(1) TEU; Declaration 1.

[22] Once the treaty comes into force, the Charter will re-appear in the 'L' series of the Official Journal. The explanatory memorandum will be left behind in the 'C' series, where it belongs.

[23] Protocol No. 30 on the application of the Charter of Fundamental Rights to Poland and to the United Kingdom; Declarations 61 and 62.

the British and Polish national parliaments, although its relevance can be questioned. The European Court of Justice retains its power to interpret the Charter as it chooses in response to an application from a national court in any of the other twenty-five states. The Court's jurisprudence on the Charter is bound to be taken into account by British and Polish courts acting in good faith to uphold the integrity of EU law.

The treaty provides a new legal basis for the Union to accede to the ECHR.[24] The Council will decide to negotiate accession to the Convention by unanimity, with the consent of European Parliament and the approval of the states. This reform meets a long-standing complaint of certain national parliaments and courts concerning the potential disjunction between the European Court of Justice in Luxembourg and the European Court of Human Rights in Strasbourg. It has been a curious anomaly that although every member state is and has to be a signatory to the ECHR, the Union itself has not been. In reaction to an approach by the German constitutional court in 1994, the European Court of Justice had concluded that the EU lacked the competence to accede in its own right to the ECHR.[25] Once the EU is signed up to the ECHR, Strasbourg will act as the external supervisor of the Luxembourg court's jurisprudence in the field of the classical fundamental rights. The relationship between the two courts will be identical to that of Strasbourg's relationship with national supreme courts – in other words, fairly amicable.

Great care has been taken to ensure that the EU's Charter should not compete with the ECHR. Consistency and conformity between the two is essential. But the EU has

---

[24] Article 6(2) TEU and Protocol No. 8 on the accession of the Union to the European Convention on the Protection of Human Rights and Fundamental Freedoms; Declaration 2.
[25] Opinion 2/94, concerning a case brought in the Bundesverfassungsgericht by Manfred Brunner against the Treaty of Maastricht. 1996 ECR 1-1759.

21

come to the view that the scope of the Charter should be broader and its thrust more modern than that of the older document. There is no good reason why the Union should not develop over time a superior fundamental rights regime, providing more extensive protection, to that of the Council of Europe.

Democratic life

In addition to the Charter, the concept of EU citizenship, first introduced by Maastricht, is affirmed and developed by the new treaty. And as we discuss further below, the right of citizens to approach the Court of Justice is broadened.[26]

The constitutional Convention was in large part a parliamentary forum. In a striking contrast with previous Intergovernmental Conferences, therefore, the positive argument for the development of European parliamentary democracy was able to be delivered directly by those with a vested interest, namely Members of the European Parliament. Never before had the systematic case for a stronger European Parliament been put – and heard – inside official circles with such force.

However, it was not only the Euro MPs in the Convention who argued for more power for Parliament. Others, especially national MPs from integrationist minded political parties, took the view that, left to their own devices, national governments would continue to fail to reverse public disquiet about the EU. Aware of the limitations of national parliaments in influencing, let alone setting, the EU's political agenda, the Convention took the bold decisions to extend European Parliamentary powers with relative ease. Those democratic advances have been carried over into Lisbon. With the new treaty in place, it will be absurd for the self-styled eurosceptics to lambast the Union for being essentially undemocratic. Even a casual reading of the treaty will reassure the citizen that the notion of the Union as some

---

[26] Article 263 TFEU.

vast, undemocratic, over-centralising plot is merely a nationalistic caricature.

The new treaty lays down three democratic principles which inform the system of government of the EU. The Union shall observe the republican principle of democratic equality between its citizens. Each citizen will 'receive equal attention' from the institutions.[27] The features of representative democracy are spelled out: citizens are represented directly in the European Parliament while the states are represented directly in the Council, which also enjoys democratic legitimacy.[28] The treaty also seeks to boost the role of the European political parties.

The party groups in the European Parliament work quite well. They ensure that Parliament's political and legislative decisions are genuinely transnational, and they make the workings of the Parliament surprisingly smooth. But the roots of this EU level party activity are shallow. The existing transnational party formations – such as the European People's Party, the European Socialists, and the European Liberal Democrat and Reform party – are loose federations of national political parties. Post-national parliamentary democracy lacks, for the moment, one essential sinew, that is, popular party forces that can articulate fluently the fears and hopes of the citizen and direct them to the top level of government.

A Statute of European Political Parties was enacted in 2002, at the height of the Convention, laying out the legal framework and financial conditions for this much-needed development to take place. In 2007 it was agreed to establish party political foundations for research and education. The new law on political parties foreseen by the Lisbon treaty should build on these foundations.[29]

---

[27] Article 9 TEU.
[28] Article 10 TEU.
[29] Article 224 TFEU.

Lisbon introduces an important novelty in the field of participatory democracy.[30] It grants the right to one million citizens coming from a 'significant' number of member states to make an 'appropriate' proposal for a new legal act to the Commission. A law is to be promulgated to specify how precisely this citizens' initiative will work. Drawn from both Swiss and American experience, the introduction of this form of direct democracy has much potential to engage the citizens in law making at the federal level. In a Union of 500 million people a petition of one million is far from being an unreasonable hurdle. Special interest organisations of civil society count their fee-paying membership in millions, and many of these nationally based bodies are collaborating closely with like-minded organisations across Europe. Trades unions and the churches might also be expected to explore the use of this new instrument. The new delimitation of competences as set out in the treaty should help the Commission to cope.

The new treaty provides for open, transparent and regular dialogue with civil society, broad consultations by the Commission with concerned parties, and an enhanced social dialogue with employers and workers organisations. The existence of the tripartite summits with the social partners is enshrined in the treaty.[31] Existing treaty commitments to taking decisions as openly and as closely to the citizens as possible are repeated.

Open government

Lisbon will introduce a much greater openness into the proceedings of the EU institutions, in particular the Council of Ministers. This was at first resisted by certain governments who hankered after the old-style diplomatic role of the Council and feared a lurch towards rendering the Council too evidently the second chamber of a bicameral federal legislature.

---

[30] Articles 11 TEU and 24 TFEU.
[31] Article 152 TFEU.

The new spirit of transparency should help the Brussels press corps to be more discerning in reporting national government positions which are frequently exaggerated by ministers and their spokesmen, with a consequent loss of focus on the common European interest. Battlefield cries defy the true nature of Council meetings, which are generally more reasonable than the language of defeats and victories implies. Experience of the very public Convention suggests that ministers begin to settle on reaching a conclusion once they know they are under scrutiny. Above all, it matters for democratic reasons that the public can find out how their government argues and votes towards the closure of the law making process. Ministers are no different from their fellow law makers, the MEPs, in this respect.

Associated with the debate about opening up the proceedings of the Council was the question of access to official documents. There has been a running squabble between the European Parliament on the one hand and the Commission and Council on the other about how liberal to be about putting working papers, at various stages of completion, into the public domain. National practices differ widely in this regard, and it is taking time for the Council and Commission to settle on an EU regime which commands respect for openness and retains necessary confidentiality. What would be a closed document in one state would be open in another. As is well known, a number of 'whistle-blowers' have emerged from the Brussels corridors, with variable degrees of credibility, to remind Parliament and press that all is not always as it seems.

The Lisbon treaty provides for a new law which will lay down the principles and limits which, on the grounds of public or private interest, should govern the right of access to documents – not only from the Commission, Council and Parliament but from all the EU's bodies, offices and agencies, and whatever the medium.[32] A similar approach is taken in

---

[32] Article 15 TFEU.

Lisbon to the protection of personal data.[33] An independent
authority is to be established to monitor the application of
the rules.

The new treaty consolidates the status of the
Ombudsman.[34] Since the establishment of the post in 1995,
the Ombudsman has played an influential part in raising
awareness within the institutions of the importance of good
administration.[35] The Ombudsman goes some way in meeting
the complaint that the treaty provides few quick, cost-
effective or non-judicial remedies for the citizen whose
interests have been abused by the EU institutions and their
agencies (including national, regional and local government
when executing EU law and policy). Lisbon means that the
Ombudsman cannot be marginalised, even by the European
Parliament which elects him. His existence is of special
significance for the newer member states where standards of
probity and efficiency in public administration have yet to
excel.

An oddity, inserted by the Convention only towards the
end of its proceedings, is a clause that elevates the status of
churches and non-confessional organisations.[36] It was a
difficult task to bridge the cultural divide between France's
aggressive laicism, forged at the Revolution, and the pious
elements to be found in several national constitutions, such
as those of Greece, Ireland and Poland, where the church
enjoys a very privileged status. The solution found by the
Convention was, in the end, quite proper. It applied the
useful Catholic principle of subsidiarity. The treaty 'respects
and does not prejudice' the national status of churches and
faith communities. The Union will maintain an open,
transparent and regular dialogue with the churches.

It is greatly to be hoped that European Islam engages
fully in the processes of citizenship and constitutional

---

[33] Articles 39 TEU and 16 TFEU.
[34] Article 228 TFEU.
[35] Jacob Söderman (1995-2003) and Nikos Diamandouros (2003-).
[36] Article 17 TFEU.

democracy. Certainly it is in the interests of Turkish and Balkan aspirations to EU membership that Muslims participate strongly in the inter-faith dialogue envisaged under the new treaty.

To placate the humanists and freemasons another, fairly bizarre, sub-clause was added to provide that the Union 'equally respects' (but not so equally that it 'does not prejudice') the status of 'philosophical and non-confessional organisations'.

CHAPTER THREE   WHAT THE UNION CAN AND CANNOT DO

Having established the values and principles that motivate the purposes of the Union, and having installed a regime of fundamental rights, the treaty proceeds to lay down the competences of the Union and the principles which govern their use.[37] It asserts the principle that the Union's competences are conferred on it by the member states and that competences not so conferred remain with the states. This helps our understanding of the European Union in two respects. First, it combats the suspicion – hard to prove but widely shared – that the EU level acquires competences almost subversively by dint of Commission aggrandisement or by inference of the judgments of the Court. Insistence on conferred competence in the treaty puts an end to any possibility of inferred competence. Second, the fact that competences are explicitly conferred on the Union to achieve specific objectives makes it easier to interpret the principle of subsidiarity, whereby competences are exercised at the lowest possible level of government compatible with efficacy.

Subsidiarity is itself redefined in the treaty to embrace the regional and local levels of governance. Concomitant to subsidiarity is the key principle of proportionality, whereby EU action should be proportionate to the scale of the problem that it seeks to address. The tendency of past Commissions to use large hammers to crack small nuts has to be avoided if the EU is to become identified with better law-making. Applying the principle of proportionality features prominently in the jurisprudence of the Court of Justice, whereas the judges have tended to regard subsidiarity as a

---

[37] Article 5 TEU.

political device requiring political rather than judicial solutions.

There was a long debate in the Convention and the two subsequent IGCs about how to classify competences. Nobody argued for a power of general competence to be given to the European Union. Some who hailed from a classical federalist background, notably representatives of the German Bundesrat, argued at first that there should be a complete catalogue of detailed vertical competences – that is, dividing functions between multi-layered governance in each relevant policy sector. That approach would have implied the need for an article spelling out states' residuary competences, the drafting of which would have been no simple task. Another approach, preferred by the Commission, argued that competences should be set out in a way that demonstrated more directly the intensity of EU level action in each field. In the end, however, it was decided to settle for a definition based on the existing treaties and jurisprudence, designed to assist comprehension and interpretation, but leaving a degree of flexibility in the arrangements to allow both for national diversity and for the present still formative state of integration. The European Parliament pushed to get real innovation in this area so as to avoid the current necessity to engage in an archaeological dig through the treaties every time it was necessary to discover what the Union can and cannot do.

The new treaty therefore introduces a clear and precise delimitation of competences conferred on the Union by member states.[38] The Union enjoys three categories of competence: exclusive, shared or complementary, and supporting or supplementary.

---

[38] Articles 2-6 TFEU and Protocol No. 25 on the exercise of shared competence.

EXCLUSIVE COMPETENCES	SHARED COMPETENCES	SUPPLEMENTARY COMPETENCES
competition rules necessary for the functioning of the internal market	social policy	industry
monetary policy (for the eurozone)	economic, social and territorial cohesion	culture
conservation of marine biological resources (under common fisheries policy)	agriculture and fisheries (excluding marine biological resources)	tourism
common commercial policy	environment	education, vocational training, youth and sport
international agreements consequent on EU law or internal competence	consumer protection	civil protection
	transport	administrative cooperation
	trans-European networks	
	energy	
	area of freedom, security and justice	
	common safety concerns in public health	
	research and technological development	
	space	
	development cooperation	

In the cases of R&D, space policy and development cooperation, EU action does not have the effect of preventing the exercise of national competence.

In addition, states will coordinate their economic and employment policies within the framework and according to the disciplines of the Union. The Union is also competent to define and implement common foreign, security and defence policies.

Exclusive competences

Where it enjoys exclusive competence, the Union has the power either to legislate itself or to empower member states to do so. The purpose of exclusive competence is to establish uniformity and to avoid risk of distorting the single market. Yet the choice of exclusive competences was not entirely uncontroversial, and certainly not unimportant as in their application exclusive competences are privileged under EU law of not being subject to the application of the principle of subsidiarity.[39] Nor is enhanced co-operation between a core group of states to be permitted in the field of exclusive competence.[40]

No previous EU Treaty had spelt out what the exclusive competences were, so the Convention had to codify a large corpus of EU case law and well-established practice. The presumption made is that exclusive competences have a basic value to the development of Europe's economic integration; that they are prerequisites of the Union and lynchpins of the *'acquis communautaire'*; and that they cannot feasibly be shared with states. Yet the fact that these competences are exclusive to the EU means neither that they are inevitably the most important competences currently possessed by the EU nor that the states have no role whatsoever to play. For example, the Union's exclusive competence in competition policy does not eliminate national competition rules but, rather, obliges them to conform to the discipline of the European single

---

[39] Article 5(3) TEU.
[40] Article 20(1) TEU.

market. There have been a number of cases brought before the Court of Justice where the Commission's attribution of exclusivity to the harmonisation of national laws in the field of the internal market has been successfully challenged.[41]

The inclusion of marine conservation in the list of exclusive competences looks mightily odd, and offends Scottish Nationalists, but the Convention and the IGCs were of the view that, for the sake of conserving stocks, the Commission and Council needed to keep full control over the size of the fishing catch.

The question of international agreements is more complicated still. As long ago as 1971 the Court ruled that, as regards common commercial policy, the EU has exclusive competence to enter into external agreements once it has adopted a common internal rule.[42] Problems arose over the interpretation of how wide the jurisdiction of the EU should be in relation to mixed international agreements involving issues that were only partly within its exclusive competence and partly enjoyed concurrently with states. Controversy persisted because whereas EU trade in goods is subject to qualified majority voting (QMV) in the Council, trade in services is not. The Commission is joined by member states in WTO negotiations in services, transport and intellectual property. The French government has been particularly insistent that this distinction should not be blurred.

Nevertheless, the Lisbon treaty will strengthen the exclusive competence of the Union in respect of international agreements that stem from EU legislation, that enable the Union to exercise its internal competence or that affect the scope of EU common rules. This threefold provision is broader than the current definition of Nice which merely implies a link between internal and external competence. Specifically, Lisbon expands the scope of the Union's competence over external economic relations to include

---

[41] For example, on tobacco advertising.

[42] Case 22/70, *ERTA* [1971], ECR 263, confirmed by subsequent case law.

foreign direct investment and the commercial aspects of intellectual property.[43]

THE ACQUIS COMMUNAUTAIRE

The 'acquis communautaire' is the name officially given to the corpus of treaties, laws, acts and jurisprudence that has built up since the foundation of the European Coal and Steel Community in 1952. It is this acquis which must be assimilated by any country that wishes to join the Union.

There have been 18 EU treaties themselves, excluding Lisbon. There are about 3500 international treaties between the EU and third countries. Roughly 25,000 legal acts are currently in force, including about 6000 classical laws, 4500 minor or delegated laws, and 2500 soft law instruments.

---

[43] Article 207 TFEU (ex-Article 133 TEC).

Shared competences

The most common category is that of shared competences. These are competences attributed to the Union but shared with states, and where both the Union and the states may adopt laws and regulations. The states shall exercise their competences in these areas only where the EU has not exercised its competence, or has decided to stop exercising it. This is the case with all the sectoral common policies where it is intended that the Union should concentrate on resolving cross-border problems, on setting minimum standards and on eliminating barriers to trade. However, in accordance with the principles of subsidiarity and proportionality, the Union institutions are impelled to seek, find and formulate in legislative or regulatory terms the added value of taking action at the Union level.

Whereas the Treaty on European Union defines the broad categories of competences, the Treaty on the Functioning of the Union lays out in much greater detail the objectives of the common policies and the role of the EU institutions in both formulating and implementing them.

In the controversial field of social policy, the EU is prohibited from harmonising national laws concerning social security.[44] In the field of public health, EU legislation is permissible to protect the trade in drugs, blood and organs, in veterinary and phytosanitary measures, and in order to combat serious cross-border health risks.[45] In both these cases, the adoption of EU law does not prevent a state from imposing higher standards of social welfare policy as long as national law is compatible with the EU treaty.

Special provisions are made with respect to two policies: research and development and international development. The preservation of national particularities is considered so important in these fields that the existence of common EU policies must not be allowed to preclude the maintenance of individual state policies.

---

[44] Article 153 TFEU.
[45] Article 168 TFEU.

Equally defiant of the conventional classification of the Union's concurrent competence were its competences in the fields of economic policy or foreign and security policy. In both cases the British government was in the vanguard of those who sought to limit the conferral of competence on the Union to the minimum extent possible. While conceding that national economic and foreign policies had to be co-ordinated at EU level, the UK wished to emphasise that the policies would continue to be conducted by national governments. One may question – and many did – whether this was, in fact, an appropriate emphasis to be making when the economic performance of the EU was plainly faltering and the fruits of common foreign and security policy were mainly risible. Earlier drafts had been both more fluent and more decisive in giving the Union powers to co-ordinate national policies.

However one might regret the back-tracking, a number of things are fairly clear. First, the Union enjoys under the treaty the competence to co-ordinate national policies, and has instruments to deploy in pursuit of co-ordination. Second, co-ordination in the economic and employment sphere is not confined to members of the eurogroup. Third, the EU is instructed to devise guidelines for national economic and employment policies. Fourth, the imperative of a common foreign and security policy is without limitation and may well lead to common defence.

Supplementary competences

The treaty designates seven policy sectors as supporting, co-ordinating or supplementary competences where the Union may support member state action without superseding it. In all such cases, the Union's legally binding acts shall not entail harmonisation of national laws or regulations. Nevertheless, growing concern about the comparative weakness of public administration in several of the accession states led to the important addition of 'administrative co-operation' as an area into which the EU has potential to develop its role.

36

Powerful lobbies in the Convention and the IGCs insisted that tourism could not be treated like any other industry, and that sport also deserved its own specific legal base in the treaty. If Lisbon enters into force before 2012, the EU will have no excuse for failing to help out with the London Olympics. Indeed, Union action in these areas often has a high relevance for local authorities, universities as well as the general public. More emphasis on developing a European cultural policy may even reap dividends in terms of public opinion.

Flexibility

There is also an important flexibility clause to allow the Union to acquire powers to attain agreed objectives where the treaties do not already provide them. It should be stressed that this clause, Article 308 TFEU, does not allow the EU to interfere in any way it fancies, but only in strictly defined circumstances in pursuit of a treaty objective. A decision to deploy the article has to be by unanimity and subject to the subsidiarity test of national parliaments; and it may not be used to blur the distinction between shared and supplementary competences. Its advantage is not that it may be used to avoid the necessity of a major constitutional amendment but in order to provide the possibility to act in circumstances that the authors of the treaty did not foresee.

In the past, the provision has been used to smooth the introduction of the euro, to prepare countries to fulfil the conditions for membership, and as a legal basis for contractual ties with third countries. It has allowed the EU to fill in some gaps in the Union's functional powers pending future treaty revisions, particularly during the building of the complex edifice of the single market.

Lisbon makes explicit what has always been implicit. Article 308 can be used only to increase the powers of the institutions but not the competences of the Union. Powers can also be returned by the EU to states. And the clause may not be deployed to attain an objective in foreign and security policy.

The renegotiation of the constitutional treaty after 2005 resulted in a tighter definition of EU competence in the field of family law, public health and personal data protection. Here, there was an 'easing of obligations' in the treaty which reflected the safeguard provisions for national security that had been built into secondary EU law since the drafting of the original constitutional treaty. It was also expressly stated in treaty form that EU competences can be reduced as well as expanded. [46]

But the changes were not all reactionary. Lisbon broke important new ground for the EU in creating legal bases in environmental policy in order to combat climate change, and in extending common energy policy from the demand to the supply side of the energy market. These two are substantive improvements to the 2004 text, reflecting the rapidly growing salience of these issues in EU policy making.

In summary, therefore, and in comparison with Nice, Lisbon will introduce new legal bases for intellectual property rights, sport, space, tourism, civil protection and administrative cooperation.[47] Environment policy has been bolstered by a reference to combating climate change.[48] Energy policy has been strengthened with respect to security and interconnectivity of supply and solidarity.[49] And it is codified in treaty form that enlargement policy will always need to take into account the Copenhagen criteria of 1993 which established the thresholds for membership.[50]

With regard to the economic and monetary policy, the Commission's role in the excessive deficit procedure is enhanced.[51] Whereas free competition is no longer written into an article of the treaty as one of the official objectives of the Union, the status of competition policy is undiminished

---

[46] Article 48(2) TEU; Declaration 18.
[47] Respectively, Articles 118, 165, 189, 195, 196, 197 TFEU.
[48] Article 191 TFEU.
[49] Article 194 TFEU.
[50] Article 49 TEU.
[51] Article 126 TFEU.

because if its reappearance in a protocol.[52] Otherwise, the economic governance of the Union is adjusted modestly to give more autonomy of action to the eurogroup, including in international financial institutions.[53] A new legal base is created for the broad economic policy guidelines, which should allow for strengthened monitoring and reporting.[54] A specific legal basis is introduced for services of general economic interest.[55]

Lastly, new horizontal clauses ensure that, in the definition and implementation of its policies, the Union will take into account gender equality, the social dimension of the single market, the combating of discrimination, sustainable development, consumer protection and animal welfare.[56]

The consolidation and classification of competences plus the extension of specific legal bases make it unlikely that the flexibility clause will need to be much used. In any case, use of the flexibility clause alongside the principle of conferred competences will naturally be subject to judicial review by the Court of Justice. Its very existence might well discourage the Court from being tempted in its case law to infer a creeping transfer of competence by other routes. A notable improvement in the new formulation is that it provides for the actual consent of the European Parliament whereas Article 308 merely allows for its consultation. MEPs have tended previously to oppose extensive use of this article because it provided neither for QMV in Council nor for co-decision with Parliament. The Commission can be expected to be less keen on its deployment in the future, given that it requires the unanimous agreement of an improbable twenty-seven ministers.

No federal system has a system of delimiting competences that is perfect. Grey areas about who does what tend to persist, and are frequently subject to adjudication by

---

[52] Protocol No. 27 on the Internal Market and Competition.
[53] Articles 137-138 TFEU.
[54] Article 136 TFEU.
[55] Article 14 TFEU; Protocol No. 26 on services of general interest.
[56] Articles 8-13 TFEU.

the supreme court. Overall, the Lisbon treaty does a good job in setting out the competences of the Union in a logical fashion. Its drafters were certainly seized of the dilemma that some citizens wanted the EU to play a greater role in some areas and a reduced role in others. It is to be hoped that Lisbon will enable the Union to concentrate on its essential tasks, to intensify action where necessary, to lighten its interventions where possible – and in all cases to justify itself to its citizens.

CHAPTER FOUR   WHO DOES WHAT

General misunderstanding of what the Union is for is nothing compared to the almost universal confusion about the role of the institutions. The Lisbon treaty describes for the first time the goal of the institutions as being to promote the Union's values and advance its objectives, to serve the interests of the Union, its citizens and member states, while ensuring the consistency, effectiveness and continuity of its policies and actions.[57]

Having named the institutions – European Parliament, European Council, Council of Ministers, European Commission, Court of Justice, European Central Bank and the Court of Auditors, in that order – the treaty lays down that they should practise mutual sincere co-operation.[58] From this we can infer that the institutions are not self-serving, that they are all grounded in the Treaty, and that they form something of a team with joint responsibility for the good governance of the Union, while respecting their own and each others' functions. In short-hand, and somewhat euphemistically, this is called 'the institutional balance'.

Subsequent clauses describe in succinct form the functions and composition of the different institutions as well as their interaction in the reformed procedures for the budget, law making, political control and consultation.[59] A second tier of institutional rules, in which the working methods of each institution are more precisely elaborated, is to be found in their own Rules of Procedure.[60]

---

[57] Article 13(1) TEU.

[58] Article 13(2). One has to assume that the Court of Justice is absolved from this last stricture.

[59] Articles 14-19 TEU.

[60] The current rules of procedure of the Commission and Parliament can be accessed fairly simply via the Europa web site, www.europa.eu. The current rules of procedure of the Council of

European Parliament

Overall, among the institutions, it is the European Parliament that stands most to gain from the entry into force of the Treaty of Lisbon. Under the key Article 294 TFEU, Parliament now becomes the co-equal legislator with the Council for almost all European laws (as foreseen by the constitutional treaty). Particularly important is the extension of the ordinary legislative procedure into agriculture, fisheries, transport and structural funds, and into the whole of the currently intergovernmental 'third pillar' of justice and interior affairs. Parliament gains law making power over totally new areas such as the citizens' initiative[61], a European space programme[62] and humanitarian aid[63]. It gains it in areas where the Parliament is at present only consulted, notably the Common Agricultural Policy and Common Fisheries Policy[64], border controls, asylum and immigration[65], and staff regulations[66]. And it gains it in areas where the Parliament has had previously no say at all, such as movement of capital to and from third countries[67], and the common commercial policy[68].

According to another key Article 314 TFEU, the new budgetary procedure ensures full parity between Parliament and Council for approval of the whole annual budget (the distinction between compulsory and non-compulsory CAP expenditure is abolished). The multi-annual financial

---

Ministers are to be found in OJ L 285, 16-10-2006. Pending its grounding in the Constitution, the rules of procedure of the European Council do not, as yet, exist.
[61] Articles 11 TEU and 24 TFEU.
[62] Article 189 TFEU.
[63] Article 214 TFEU.
[64] Article 43 TFEU.
[65] Articles 77-79 TFEU.
[66] Article 336 TFEU.
[67] Article 64 TFEU.
[68] Article 207 TFEU.

framework, which becomes legally binding, also has to be agreed by Parliament.[69]

MEPs are elected every five years: the election on 4-7 June 2009 will be its seventh.[70] According to the new treaty, the Parliament will consist of 751 MEPs, although because of its non-ratification, Parliament will start the next mandate with only 736 MEPs. The treaty introduces the principle of degressive proportionality for the apportionment of parliamentary seats between six for the smallest states and 96 for the largest. Ironically, the degressive principle was immediately breached by the IGC, which gave one seat too many to Italy for the term 2009-14.[71] MEPs will henceforward represent 'the Union's citizens' rather than 'the peoples of the States'.[72]

Given the impact of enlargement on the Parliament, the stability of the party groups has been impressive. Although enlargement led to a slight decrease in the dominance of the European People's Party (EPP) and the Party of European Socialists (PES) – and a rise in numbers for the Liberals – the three large groups together accounted for 73 per cent of the MEPs in 1999 and 77 per cent ten years later. Four small groups attract 20 per cent of the House, with a tiny remainder of non-attached Members, too wayward to be grouped at all.

The new treaty codifies the Statute of Members of the European Parliament, a hugely controversial piece of legislation that took many years to accomplish. At present MEPs are paid the same as their respective national MPs, leading to a situation in which the ratio of a Hungarian MEP's salary to that of an Italian is 1:14. From July 2009 a package of measures will come into force that includes a common salary, taxation and pension scheme plus a

---

[69] Article 312 TFEU.
[70] Article 14 TEU.
[71] Declaration 4.
[72] Article 189 TEC.

straightforward system for the reimbursement of travel and other expenses.[73]

The treaty also provides for a law to regulate political parties at the EU level, and lays down Parliament's powers to set up committees of inquiry, to receive petitions from the citizen, to appoint the European Ombudsman, and to adopt its own Rules of Procedure by a majority of its component Members. Parliament will normally act under the treaty by a simple majority of the votes cast except where the treaty provides otherwise, as at the second reading stage of the ordinary legislative procedure.

While the Commission remains responsible for the formal drafting and introduction of a law, MEPs can exert real political pressure on the Commission to act even when it is unwilling to do so. If the Commission declines to follow Parliament's lead it has to justify its decision before Parliament.[74] Crucially, Parliament gains the right under the treaty to initiate in future revision of the treaty itself.[75] That is a highly significant step forward towards the constitutionalisation of the European Union, ending as it would the states' monopoly over treaty change. Parliament will also be an integral part of the Convention established to change the treaty, and its consent will be necessary if there is not to be a Convention.

Parliament retains its right both to approve and to censure the whole Commission. Although Parliament does not gain the right to sack individual Commissioners, it has gradually been acquiring the authority to bring individual Commissioners to book. In 2004, President-elect Barroso was unable to appoint the team of Commissioners served up

---

[73] Article 223(2) TFEU. An MEP's salary is to be set at 38.5 per cent of that of a judge of the European Court of Justice – which would give every MEP around € 7500 per month. For a good description of the struggle to agree a Members' Statute, see Julian Priestley, *Six Battles that Shaped Europe's Parliament*, John Harper, 2008.

[74] Article 225 TFEU.

[75] Article 48 TEU.

to him by the European Council because of objections raised by MEPs during informal hearings of the individual candidates. One nominee was withdrawn by her government, another resigned and a third had his portfolio switched by Mr Barroso. From the ensuing crisis emerged a new Framework Agreement between the Parliament and the Commission which provides for the day-to-day workings of the inter-institutional relationship and has greatly increased the Commission's accountability to the Parliament.[76] It was agreed that if Parliament votes by a substantial majority to withdraw confidence in an individual member of the college, the President will either ask that member to resign or he will come before Parliament to justify his refusal to do so. That concession gives MEPs the potential firing mechanism they have hitherto lacked to go for the 'nuclear option' and sack the whole college.

The European Parliament's initial rejection then later approval of the EU's new executive provoked much media comment. The reportage was such that the discerning public could see MEPs behaving exactly like it expects of parliamentarians. As for the Commission, although its confirmation in office was difficult and protracted, the college emerged strengthened. It is impossible now for critics to accuse the Commission of being unelected bureaucrats. Overall, the crisis over the approval of the Barroso Commission breathed some welcome democratic life into the constitutional process.

Under the Treaty of Lisbon the next President of the Commission will be elected by Parliament. The candidate will be proposed to MEPs by the European Council, nominated by QMV, taking into account the results of the parliamentary elections.[77] Parliament will also invest the whole

---

[76] European Parliament Resolution on the Framework Agreement, 26 May 2005. The Agreement is reproduced as Annex XIII of the Parliament's Rules of Procedure. Parliament's procedures for the appointment of the Commission appear as Annex XVIb.

[77] Article 17(7) TEU; Declaration 6 and 11.

Commission, including the High Representative for Foreign Affairs, who will also be Vice-President of the Commission.[78]

European Council

The one body that was not best pleased by the early tribulations of the Barroso Commission was the European Council, whose first selection was rejected by the Parliament. The European Council would be further tamed by the treaty under which it is turned into a fully-fledged institution of the Union, thereby obliging the heads of government to abide by the inter-institutional rules, including the supervision of the Court of Justice. [79]

The job of the European Council, which is composed of the heads of state or government plus the President of the Commission, is to provide the Union with necessary impetus and to define its general political directions and priorities. The powers of the European Council have grown rather haphazardly over the years. The fact that the Council of Ministers has had to share more and more legislative power with the Parliament has been compensated for by the emergence of the European Council at the top of the hierarchy, which also bore witness to the growing importance of European integration to national politics. But the European Council has tended to complicate decision making at ministerial level not only by treading wilfully on prerogatives but also by providing an excuse for ministers themselves not to make progress on a problematical dossier. Whereas the other EU institutions have been required to act only within the limits of the powers conferred upon them by treaty, no such injunction applied, until Lisbon, to the European Council.[80]

Until now the chairmanship of the European Council has rotated between serving presidents or prime ministers every six months. Lisbon introduces a new 'permanent' President of the European Council (elected for two and a

---

[78] Article 18 TEU.
[79] Articles 15 TEU and 263 TFEU.
[80] Article 7 TEC and Article 263 TFEU.

half years, renewable once) who will chair and drive forward its work. He or she, who cannot remain a head of government but will probably be drawn from the fairly swollen ranks of ex-heads of government, will prepare meetings of the European Council and report to Parliament afterwards.[81] Their chief job will be the external representation of the Union at summit level, alongside – and hopefully in harmony with – the President of the Commission. Neither the Commission President nor the new-style President of the European Council will vote. How the European Council adjusts to its new situation may depend heavily on the qualities of the person selected to be its chairman.[82] After the treaty comes into force, the European Council will have to adopt its first Rules of Procedure by simple majority. One waits to see those with more than customary interest.

Council of Ministers

The Council of Ministers exercises legislative and budgetary functions jointly with the European Parliament, as well as carrying out policy-making and co-ordinating functions in those reserve areas where it shares executive powers with the Commission.

In a parallel provision to the power enjoyed by the Parliament, the Council can also invite the Commission to submit a proposal to it, legislative or otherwise, with the similar proviso that the Commission would have to justify a refusal to do so.[83]

The Council of Ministers consists of one representative of each member state government who must be able to commit that government. Apart from some important exceptions laid down in the treaty, the Council is to decide by qualified majority vote.[84] It is to meet in various policy configurations, led by a General Affairs Council. Its work is

---

[81] Article 15 TEU; Declaration 6.
[82] Article 235 TFEU.
[83] Article 241 TFEU.
[84] Article 16(3) TEU.

prepared by a powerful Committee of Permanent Representatives (COREPER).

As we have already noted, in a very important constitutional innovation, the treaty lays down that the Council will have to meet in public 'when it deliberates and votes on a draft legislative act'.[85]

Since the beginning of the European Community, the chair has rotated among states every six months. With six fairly cohesive founder member states that system achieved some continuity. With twenty-seven fairly disparate states, it is collapsing. Lisbon attempts an improvement. The sectoral Councils are to be chaired by ministers from a team of three member states for a period of eighteen months, with each of the three chairing each formation in turn for six months.[86]

The legislative process

Qualified majority voting becomes the general rule in the Council – defined as a double majority of 55 per cent of states representing 65 per cent of the population (while a minimum number of four states is needed to constitute a blocking minority).[87] Many significant items move from unanimity to QMV, including the whole of justice and interior affairs. Only the most sensitive areas remain subject to unanimity: tax, social security, citizens' rights, languages, seats of the institutions and the main lines of common foreign, security and defence policies. In some of these areas, such as anti-discrimination measures, Parliament gains the right of consent.[88] And in others, such as ecological taxation, specific *passerelles* to allow the Union to cross from abnormal procedures to the ordinary legislative procedure are inserted.[89]

The extension of QMV plus co-decision will unblock decision making especially in the policy field of freedom,

---

[85] Article 16(8) TEU.
[86] Articles 16(9) TEU, 236 TFEU; Declaration 9.
[87] Articles 16(4) TEU and 238 TFEU.
[88] Article 19 TFEU as compared to Article 13 TEC.
[89] Article 192(2) TFEU.

security and justice. Recourse to the lowest common denominator should become less frequent as the injection of real party politics via the greater involvement of the European Parliament will tend to make laws more substantive and less platitudinous. Recent experience – for example, with REACH, the services directive and the climate and energy package – suggests that MEPs working together can find the vital majorities for complex and controversial proposals that have evaded the Council of Ministers when left to the devices of civil servants, lawyers and diplomats.[90]

In practice, the Council votes by QMV on only about a quarter of the occasions it could do so in theory. QMV has become a mechanism of last resort, once every effort to reach a consensus has been exhausted. However, Lisbon postponed the introduction of the new system from 2009 until 2014 – and added a transitional period until 2017 during which recourse can still be had to the voting rules of the Treaty of Nice.[91] On top of all that, a new mechanism based on the 'Ioannina compromise', first introduced in 1994, will allow 55 per cent of the states which form a blocking minority (or states representing 55 per cent of the population) to ask for a delay and reconsideration of a draft law before its adoption.[92] A protocol negotiated in the last hours of the IGC, at the request of Poland, states that the Council can only amend or repeal the Ioannina clause by consensus – effectively rendering this new delaying

---

[90] In 2006 REACH regulated the use of chemicals across the Union, in 2007 the services sector was gradually opened up to the single market, and in 2008 the climate and energy package was passed to achieve a reduction in carbon emissions. In all these cases Parliament came to the rescue of the draft laws which had stuck in the Council.

[91] Article 16(5) TEU and Articles 3 and 4 of Protocol No. 36 on transitional provisions.

[92] Declaration 7. The Ioannina compromise was first introduced in 1994 at the request of Spain and the UK and lasted until the coming into force of Nice. It was used on four occasions to achieve minor amendments to a draft law, the historic importance of which has been forgotten.

mechanism permanent.[93] One may wonder why all this ponderous procrastination was deemed either necessary or desirable when everyone had already agreed the decision in principle to lighten the voting procedure in the Council. It is certainly regrettable that the inclusion of the new Ioannina clause could well serve to further frustrate decision making in the Council. And nobody can claim that the decision-making processes of the Council are simple or clear, and it may become a bit embarrassing once they will be exposed to the glare of public and media scrutiny.

Lest there be scepticism about the extent of the changes wrought by Lisbon to law making in the Union, the facts are these. Under the Treaty of Nice there are 36 legal bases for the use of the ordinary legislative procedure (co-decision). Lisbon shifts a further existing 29 items to the ordinary legislative procedure, and creates 26 new items which will be decided by the ordinary legislative procedure, totalling 91.[94] The ordinary legislative procedure will not be used in 76 cases. Under Lisbon the Council will act by QMV in 154 cases, an increase of 22 on Nice, and the Council will act under a special procedure short of unanimity in a further nine cases, totalling 163. The Council will act by unanimity in 58 cases.

The EU could not have made as much democratic progress as it has unless its recent experience of co-decision had proved fruitful. The role of the European Commission is crucial to the success of the ordinary legislative procedure. In the first place, the Commission launches the legislative proposal. It can withdraw it at any stage up to, but not including, conciliation. The Commission also retains the right to re-launch a defeated proposal on its own initiative in the future. During the second reading, where the Commission

---

[93] Protocol No. 9 on the Decision of the Council relating to the implementation of Article 16(4) TEU and Article 238(2) TFEU between 1 November 2014 and 31 March 2017 on the one hand, and as from 1 April 2017 on the other.

[94] This compares with 15 cases of co-decision when first introduced by the Treaty of Maastricht.

gives a negative opinion on a proposed amendment from Parliament, Council has to act by unanimity to approve it. Once into the conciliation process the Commission's job is not to press its own proposal but to broker agreement between Parliament, acting by an absolute majority of half its membership, and Council, acting by QMV. Following the recent enlargement the official conciliation committee has grown to an improbable size for a negotiating team, with twenty-seven members on each side. So the role of the Commission as facilitator in a smaller and informal 'trialogue' has become even more important.

Nevertheless, it would be a mistake to think of the Commission as being a completely free agent with respect to its right of initiative. Governments, MEPs, industry and NGOs all play their part in influencing a Commission decision to launch new legislation. The Commission has a freer hand when it comes to choosing between different types of legal act. In 2005, for example, the Commission downgraded a measure on animal welfare to a recommendation out of respect for the principle of subsidiarity. And the Commission has refused to entertain making a legislative proposal in the treacherous territory of media law.

The Commission has also taken seriously its obligation to undertake and publish impact assessments of its draft laws with respect to finance, bureaucracy and the environment. Although subject to regular criticism from the Council and Parliament about the quality of these assessments, the Commission has become much more thorough and systematic in exercising legislative self-restraint than either the Council or Parliament.

During the term of the fifth legislature (1999-2004), 403 legislative acts were adopted under the co-decision procedure. 124 of those concerned the harmonisation of national laws in order to boost the single market.[95] The next most common areas for use of the co-decision procedure

---

[95] Under the legal base of Article 95 TEC.

51

after legal harmonisation were environment policy, maritime and air transport, public health, the right of establishment and common statistics policies. Only two directives failed – concerning company takeovers and access to port services – when MEPs rejected at third reading the compromises reached in the conciliation committee. Roughly speaking, a quarter of the draft acts were agreed at first reading and half at second reading, while the remaining quarter become subject to conciliation. About half of the amendments tabled by Parliament found their way into the final law.

In the current legislature (2004-09) the number of laws agreed at first reading has increased dramatically. Between July 2004 and the time of writing, 438 legislative acts were concluded under co-decision: 321 of those at first reading, 94 at second and only 23 after conciliation (at third reading). In July 2005, Parliament took the unprecedented step of defeating a directive – on the patenting of computer-implemented inventions – at second reading. In the case of first and second reading agreements almost all Parliament's amendments are passed into law. Nevertheless, the current fashion for hasty first reading deals risks sacrificing good quality law making. It also elevates the role of the Commission in the vital but opaque informal trialogues, as well as annoying those national parliaments which are not geared up to tracking at close quarters the faster moving EU legislative processes. MEPs should not forget that their own strength is maximised when the full co-decision procedure is played out.

Ordinary Legislative Procedure
Article 294 TFEU
Parliament normally acts by simply majority; Council normally acts by QMV

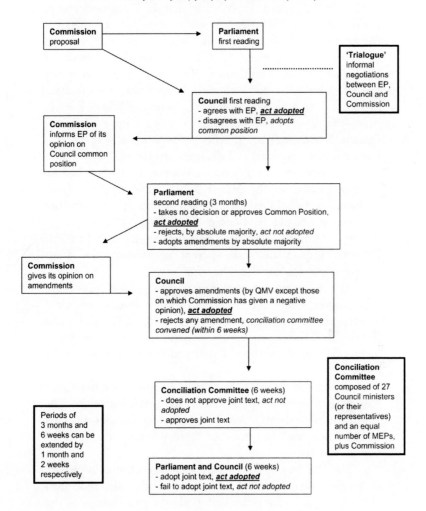

Commission
proposal

Parliament
first reading

'Trialogue'
informal negotiations between EP, Council and Commission

Council first reading
- agrees with EP, ***act adopted***
- disagrees with EP, *adopts common position*

Commission
informs EP of its opinion on Council common position

Parliament
second reading (3 months)
- takes no decision or approves Common Position, ***act adopted***
- rejects, by absolute majority, *act not adopted*
- adopts amendments by absolute majority

Commission
gives its opinion on amendments

Council
- approves amendments (by QMV except those on which Commission has given a negative opinion), ***act adopted***
- rejects any amendment, *conciliation committee convened (within 6 weeks)*

Conciliation Committee (6 weeks)
- does not approve joint text, *act not adopted*
- approves joint text

Conciliation Committee
composed of 27 Council ministers (or their representatives) and an equal number of MEPs, plus Commission

Periods of 3 months and 6 weeks can be extended by 1 month and 2 weeks respectively

Parliament and Council (6 weeks)
- adopt joint text, ***act adopted***
- fail to adopt joint text, *act not adopted*

Rationalisation

In addition to establishing co-decision as the norm, the new treaty manages to simplify the procedure, and to lay it out better.[96] It is made crystal clear that the Parliament enjoys parity with the Council at each stage of law-making. Furthermore, Lisbon entirely suppresses the current 'cooperation procedure'.[97] Use of another abnormal procedure, where the Council decides after receiving the formal opinion of the Parliament (called the 'consultation' procedure), is reduced in number to twenty. While its powers of co-decision widen, Parliament's formal right of assent (renamed 'consent') in specific circumstances is retained – mostly for international and financial agreements.

It is estimated by Parliament's services that had Lisbon been in force over the period 2004-07 the number of co-decision laws would have risen from 301 to 517, the number of consents would have risen from 58 to 190, while the number of consultations would have fallen from 492 to 144. Lisbon's impact on the internal organisation of both Parliament and Council will be large.

The increased use of the ordinary legislative procedure will reduce the need for ad hoc 'inter-institutional agreements' between the Commission, Council and Parliament. However, the treaty still provides for inter-institutional agreements of a practical nature, which may be binding.[98]

In addition, MEPs will still pass formal 'resolutions', the European Council presidency will still produce its 'conclusions' and the Council of Ministers will still make its 'communications', but none of these will have the force of Union legislation.

The Parliament, for its part, has always voted in plenary in public, often with roll call votes so that the individual choices of MEPs are published. Only the proceedings of the

---

[96] Article 251 TEC which has become Article 294 TFEU.
[97] Article 252 TEC.
[98] Article 295 TFEU.

conciliation committee and the associated trialogues remain closed because they are a negotiation, and conciliation would be unlikely to work efficiently if exposed to the glare of publicity. In any case, the results of the conciliation procedure are now posted quickly on the website, and all other phases of the process are public.[99]

Parallel to the work of the Convention in 2003 a new inter-institutional agreement on better law-making was painstakingly negotiated between the three institutions.[100] Its aim is to improve the timetabling and co-ordination of the legislative process as well as to sharpen the monitoring of how EU law takes effect inside member states. All the institutions involved in the ordinary legislative procedure are bound to increase the use of regulatory, financial and environmental impact assessments. The Commission, in particular, now has to justify its decision to choose the legislative route (as opposed to an executive act). It knows its justifications are being more heavily scrutinised than before by the Council, Parliament and even national parliaments. Ex-post review of EU laws and framework laws will be enhanced by the wider scope of the Court's jurisdiction.

As we have seen, although the Commission is the main executive authority of the Union, it has to share some of its executive powers with the Council of Ministers. In the Convention a tough battle was fought to reduce, if not quite eliminate, the Council's executive powers. Under the present arrangements of the Treaty of Nice, the job of the Commission is to ensure the application of the treaty and the implementation of EU policy, to help shape the decisions of the Parliament and Council, to make recommendations and issue opinions, and also to exercise certain powers conferred on it by the Council.[101] The Council enjoys executive authority in the original field of the common market not only to confer powers upon the Commission but also to take

---

[99] Rules governing public access to official documents are set out in Regulation (EC) 1049/2001.
[100] OJ C 321, 31-12-2003.
[101] Article 211 TEC.

executive decisions itself, for example, to fix agricultural prices, and to ensure co-ordination of the general economic policies of the states.[102] The Council is given the power to take decisions to ensure that the objectives set out in this treaty are attained.

The Treaty of Lisbon makes progress in clarifying who could delegate executive authority to the Commission and under what terms. A greater willingness on behalf of the legislator to delegate technical minutiae to the Commission has been recorded in the new treaty. 'Delegated acts', which give the Commission the power to adopt non-legislative acts of general application and to amend non-essential elements of a law, will have to be authorised in a regulation or directive, requiring the consent of both Council and Parliament. [103] The objectives, content, scope and duration of the delegation will have to be specified in the law. Essential political choices will still have to be made in the legislation itself and not in the delegated act. The institutions are committed to continuing the practice initiated in the financial services sector – the so-called Lamfalussy procedure – to consult with national experts before it drafts amendments to its executive acts in response to changed technical or market conditions.[104] Both legislative chambers also have the power to call back the delegation.

Comitology

More difficulty was experienced by the Convention in reaching agreement on how to implement legally binding acts of the Union – either regulations or decisions – inside states. The states are obliged to adopt all measures of national law necessary to ensure implementation – 'implementing acts'.[105] In theory, the Commission is responsible for overseeing the implementation of EU legal acts at the European level. In practice, of course, the Commission needs the participation

---

[102] Article 202 TEC.
[103] Article 290 TFEU.
[104] Declaration 39.
[105] Article 291 TFEU.

of the states both to formulate the necessary implementing measures and to monitor their efficacy. Since 1987, and in response to the growing use of co-decision in the area of the single market, the Union has managed the drafting of implementing measures through the 'comitology' system. There are three types of comitology committee, all composed of national government officials and all chaired by the Commission. There are almost 250 of these committees, dealing annually with about 1750 acts.

Advisory committees give the Commission maximum discretion, and have been used for fairly technical questions. Management committees oblige the Commission to refer to Council any matter where its decision differs from the view of the Committee, expressed by QMV. Council may overturn the Commission's decision, acting by QMV. This procedure is used for the management of common policies and spending programmes. Regulatory committees oblige the Commission actually to acquire the approval of the committee, acting by QMV, before taking action. If the committee fails to act, the matter is referred back to Council which can take the necessary decision by QMV. If the Council fails to act, the Commission can finally adopt the implementing measure itself unless the Council does not object by QMV. Since a revision of the system in an interinstitutional agreement of 1999, and in order to assist the scrutiny by the European Parliament of the comitology decisions, all documents are now made public and the Commission delivers an annual comitology report.

Under Lisbon, wherever uniform implementation is required it will be the Commission which is normally granted the necessary powers to ensure implementation. In some duly justified specific cases, however, including agricultural prices and fishing quotas, it will still be the Council which remains responsible.

Lisbon makes one important improvement to the existing comitology procedure.[106] At present the Council

---

[106] Article 202 TEC.

decides on the rules governing the Commission's exercise of these executive powers by unanimity, after having received the opinion of the Parliament. Today, these comitology arrangements are subject to an inter-institutional agreement. Under Lisbon, a regulation or directive enacted by the ordinary legislative procedure will be required to lay down in advance the rules and general principles concerning mechanisms for control by the states of the Commission's implementing powers.[107] In effect, Lisbon codifies a reformed comitology decision of 2006 which introduced the new procedure of 'regulatory procedure with scrutiny'. This empowers the Commission to complete the legislative process in technical or detailed ways while remaining under the watchful eye of both Council and Parliament, which have co-equal powers to call in any Commission decision. This is a big step forward for the Parliament and, by implication, a significant step forward for the Commission. It should lead to the rationalisation of the burdensome comitology system, and encourage the use of 'sunset' clauses that would mandate the legislator to review a law after a certain, specified time.

A new hierarchy of norms is established which distinguishes between legislative acts, delegated acts and implementing acts – although, confusingly, the terms 'law' and 'framework law' postulated in the 2004 constitutional treaty have been abandoned in favour of keeping the present terminology (directives, regulations and decisions). [108] As the subtle re-balancing of the comitology system illustrates, the treaty establishes a good balance between the demands of enhanced democracy and the needs of greater efficiency in a larger and more complex Union – while all the time understanding the principle of the separation of powers between legislature and executive.

In another change made by the treaty, greater emphasis will have to be placed on the principle of proportionality in the drafting of EU legal acts, either of a legislative or an

---

[107] Article 291(3) TFEU.
[108] Articles 288-292 TFEU.

executive nature.[109] Furthermore, there will have to be fully reasoned justifications for the choice of instrument on a case by case basis. And we have already noted the Commission's commitment to verify all its legislative proposals against the provisions of the Charter of Fundamental Rights.

In summary, Lisbon makes good progress in simplifying and in making more transparent the exercise of powers at the Union level. Its ultimate rejection would make things needlessly complicated all over again – to the undoubted detriment to the quality of European public policy.

The Vice-President/High Representative

The notable exception to the dizzy circus of Council presidencies is the Foreign Affairs Council which is to be chaired by the new post of the double-hatted Vice-President/High Representative, who will be appointed by the European Council with the agreement of the President of the Commission and confirmed (or not) as part of the college by the Parliament.[110]

Besides chairing the Council of foreign ministers, the High Representative will also manage a new European External Action Service, formed by a combination of national civil servants, the Council secretariat and the Commission. The External Action Service will be established by the Council with the consent of the Commission and after consulting Parliament.[111] As the External Action Service will be funded from the EU budget, MEPs will obtain significant control.

These new institutional arrangements for managing the external activities of the Union are radical improvements on the present system of Nice. The importance of the innovation of the Vice-President/High Representative should not be underestimated. He or she will bring to the field of foreign and security policy a comparable right of initiative to that enjoyed by the Commission in internal EU matters.

---

[109] Article 296 TFEU.

[110] Article 18 TEU; Declaration 6.

[111] Article 27(3) TEU; Declaration 15.

Their job will be to seek out and articulate the common interest of all member states, to persuade the Council to accept policy proposals, and to be responsible for policy implementation, using the new tool of the External Action Service. As chair of the Council of foreign ministers the Vice-President/High Representative will be responsible for brokering some difficult agreements, especially in foreign policy and security matters where unanimity is required.

He or she will be responsible to the Council for the conduct of common foreign, security and defence policy and to the Commission for the conduct of the Union's external relations. The new post will combine the current roles of the Council's High Representative for foreign and security policy, Javier Solana, (who is also Secretary-General of the Council) with that of the European Commissioner for external affairs, Benita Ferrero-Waldner.

European Commission

The European Commission retains its existing prerogatives under the Lisbon treaty, and has them spelt out comprehensively for the first time. Its job is to promote the general interest of the Union and to ensure the application of the treaty and EU law. It executes the budget and manages programmes. It initiates law. It has co-ordinating, executive and management functions, both internal and external. It is to become responsible for the programming of the work of the institutions.

The right to initiate the Union's multi-annual programme with a view to reaching either a binding or non-binding inter-institutional agreement with the Council and Parliament is an important extension of the Commission's powers.[112] It is intended to bring more strategic coherence to the work of the institutions, to improve parliamentary scrutiny and to bind together more effectively the two executive branches of the Union (Commission and Council). President Barroso is already experimenting with the first five-

---

[112] Article 17(1) TEU.

year programme. The Commission's powers to draft the Union's official work programme take precedence over the duty falling on the three governments forming the eighteen month team presidency of the Council of Ministers to have a common programme.[113]

Lisbon strengthens the powers of the Commission to enforce compliance with EU law. As soon as the Court of Justice has ruled on non-compliance, the Commission will be able to specify the amount of the fine which will be imposed automatically by the Court in the event of continued non-compliance.[114] Such a streamlined process would have brought France's refusal to import British beef in the wake of the BSE crisis to a speedy climax.

The wide extension under Lisbon of the ordinary legislative procedure offers wide potential for a Commission that has a coherent legislative programme at home and well-focussed strategies abroad. A strong Commission will exploit the democratic opportunities arising from the fact that, under Lisbon, it is to be held more accountable by MEPs than in the past. The good governance of the Union demands a strong executive, and the treaty provides for that.

The Convention and the IGCs spent many hours discussing the matter of the future size and shape of the Commission. It was agreed that members of the Commission should be chosen for a term of five years from persons of general competence, European commitment and indubitable independence. The treaty eventually laid down that the college appointed in November 2009 was to have, like the previous Barroso Commission, one member nominated by each state. The college appointed in 2014, however, was supposed to correspond to two-thirds of the number of member states, unless the European Council, acting unanimously, lost its nerve. In a decision which has come back to haunt those responsible, the treaty insists on strictly

---

[113] Declaration 9.
[114] Article 260 TFEU.

equal rotation between nationalities, thereby assuring each nationality representation in two colleges out of three.[115]

Apart from a larger role for the Parliament in his or her election, the powers of the Commission President remain substantively unchanged. The Council 'by common accord with the President-elect' will nominate the college which will then require a vote of consent by the Parliament. The President will dispose portfolios.

European Court of Justice

Under the present treaty, the European Court of Justice is enjoined, cryptically, to 'ensure that in the interpretation and application of this Treaty the law is observed'.[116] The Court's main task is to hear cases brought by the member states and the institutions against one another, and to settle disputes. But its power of judicial review is not unlimited. The treaty seeks to protect common foreign and security policy and police and judicial co-operation in criminal matters from interference by the Court. It also makes it very difficult for ordinary citizens to get redress from the Court unless they can prove they are directly and individually and adversely affected.[117]

The good news about Lisbon is that the jurisdiction of the European Court of Justice is expanded to cover all the activities of the Union with the express exception of common foreign and security policy.[118] However, the Court has oversight in the case of a breach of procedure or a conflict over competence (in effect, patrolling the frontier between the foreign and security policy and the rest of the Union's activities). The Court can hear appeals against restrictive measures and give an opinion about an international treaty.[119] Where the opinion of the Court is

---

[115] Article 17(5) TEU; Declaration 10.
[116] Article 220 TEC.
[117] Article 230 TEC.
[118] Articles 19 and 24(1) TEU.
[119] Article 275 TFEU.

adverse, the agreement envisaged may not enter into force unless it is amended or the Treaties are revised.[120]

The Treaty of Nice had already made some useful reforms of the internal structure of the EU Court system. Lisbon built on these by making three changes of terminology. The entire judicial system becomes the 'Court of Justice of the European Union'. The Court of First Instance, created in 1989 to help the Court of Justice, becomes the 'General Court'. Judicial panels become 'specialised courts'. The Court of Justice is to be composed of one judge per member state. The General Court is to have at least one judge per member state. The number of Advocates-General is increased from eight to eleven.[121] Judges and Advocates-General are to be appointed by the common accord of states for renewable terms of six years. A panel of seven former members of the Court, one of whom is appointed by the European Parliament, must be consulted over these judicial appointments.[122]

The Court's procedure on compliance has been streamlined, thereby greatly enhancing the Commission's ability to enforce compliance by states to their obligations.[123] Lisbon also makes some significant if cautious changes to the scope of jurisdiction of the Court. The requirement of individual concern will no longer be necessary in order to challenge a 'regulatory act which does not entail implementing measures'.[124] This enhances the right of an individual to approach the Court. The Committee of the Regions gains the right to address the Court in defence of its prerogatives.[125] And as we discuss later, national parliaments may approach the Court, via their governments, to protect their prerogatives under the terms of the subsidiarity protocol. There is also a useful widening of the scope of the

---

[120] Article 218(11) TFEU.
[121] Declaration 38.
[122] Article 19 TEU, Articles 253-255 TFEU.
[123] Article 260 TFEU.
[124] Article 263(4) TFEU.
[125] Article 263(3) TFEU.

Court's jurisdiction to give preliminary rulings not only on the validity and interpretation of acts of the EU institutions but also of its 'bodies, offices and agencies'.[126]

The abolition of the special 'third pillar' of justice and home affairs means that the scope of the Court's jurisdiction widens to include all actions of the Union concerning the development of the area of freedom, security and justice except that it will not have jurisdiction to review the validity or proportionality of national police and security service operations.[127] But in general the possibility for a state to choose whether or not to accept the jurisdiction of the Court in the field of police and judicial co-operation in criminal matters will be removed under Lisbon.[128]

As far as common foreign and security policy is concerned, the jurisdiction of the Court will be extended with respect of sanctions. The Court will gain the power to rule on direct or individual challenges against sanctions and other restrictive measures imposed by the Union, although it will not have jurisdiction over the common policy as such.[129] In other words, the treaty would not allow the European Parliament to sue the British government in the Court of Justice for unlawfully invading Iraq.

In general, the Court has the authority it needs to interpret the treaty. It can anticipate a rise in the volume of litigation, not least with respect to the Charter, and worries have been expressed about how expeditiously the Court will be able to dispatch justice. However, the Treaty of Nice has helped matters by allowing rulings to be made without first hearing an Opinion from an Advocate-General. This, coupled with the wide use of chambers, has made the Court much more efficient. Lisbon enables specialised courts, for instance on patent law, to be set up (with the agreement of Parliament). The EU Courts deal with a total of about 1000

---

[126] Article 267 TFEU.
[127] Article 276 TFEU.
[128] Article 35(2) TEC.
[129] Article 275 TFEU.

cases each year, a quarter of which are in the field of intellectual property.

Nevertheless, to ensure efficacy, the Court of Justice still needs to firm up the commitment of national courts to co-operate closely with it in seeking to uphold the rule of the EU treaty. For that reason the new treaty instructs member states to ensure that national judicial systems become more effectively integrated into the EU judicial system.[130]

Other bodies

The new treaty affords the status of 'institution' to the European Central Bank (ECB) and the Court of Auditors. The former, whose job it is to issue the euro and, together with national central banks to 'conduct the monetary policy of the Union', remains strongly independent. The ECB enjoys the power, as yet unused, of prudential supervision over the banking sector.[131] Members of the executive board of the European Central Bank are appointed by the European Council, acting by QMV and after consulting the Parliament, for a non-renewable term of eight years.[132]

One significant – and very sensible – change to the constitution of the Central Bank is that, under the terms of Lisbon, the President and other members of the Executive Board will be appointed by the European Council acting by QMV.[133] The current treaty stipulates 'by common accord' – which proved a very difficult mountain to climb at the time of the appointment of Wim Duisenberg, the first President, in May 1998. Another change to the benefit of the Parliament is that it gains the right to be consulted over any revision to the statute of the ECB.[134]

Against expectations, no changes were made by the Convention or the IGCs to the composition of the Court of

---

[130] Article 19(1) TEU.

[131] Article 127(6) TFEU.

[132] Articles 282 and 283 TFEU.

[133] Articles 283(2) TFEU.

[134] Article 40(2) Protocol No. 4 on the Statute of the European System of Central Banks and of the ECB.

Auditors, which remains at the increasingly inflated size of one member per state. The auditors are appointed by the Council of Ministers, acting by QMV and after consulting the European Parliament, for a renewable term of six years.[135]

Important changes are however made to the role of the European Investment Bank, notably giving it the power to take equity stakes in commercial undertakings, normally as a complement to a loan or guarantee.[136] Any public or private entity will be able to apply directly to the EIB for financing. The potential of the EIB to assist in the economic recovery of Europe is therefore enlarged substantially, and one can expect the Bank to become a key player if and when a common economic policy of the Union emerges. Founded in 1958, the EIB is already the world's top lender, larger than the IMF and the World Bank put together. It agreed loans of € 48 bn in 2008, and is expected to lend € 63 bn in 2009.

The terms of office of the Economic and Social Committee and the Committee of the Regions is extended to five years from four. Their opinions are to be forwarded directly to Parliament as well as to the Commission and Council. Neither body, despite their pleadings, made it to the elevated standing of EU institution. The Economic and Social Committee and the Committee of the Regions remain advisory bodies, composed of representatives of economic and civil society and of regional and local authorities, respectively.[137] Both bodies have 350 members and are appointed by the Council, acting unanimously on a Commission proposal.[138] The Committee of the Regions gains the right to approach the Court of Justice.[139]

---

[135] Articles 285 and 286 TFEU.
[136] Protocol No. 5 on the statute of the EIB, Article 18(2) and Article 309 TFEU.
[137] Article 300 TFEU.
[138] Articles 301 and 305 TFEU.
[139] Article 263(3) TFEU.

National parliaments

The Lisbon treaty reminds us that national governments are democratically accountable to their own parliaments.[140] Heads of government in the European Council and ministers in the Council are answerable in their national parliaments for their activities in the EU arena. If there is a 'democratic deficit' in the European Union it cannot be just the fault of the EU institutions, then, but also of national parliaments which fail, for one reason or another, to connect the citizen with the new, federal dimension of politics. To clarify matters, a new clause in the Lisbon treaty usefully collects together a description of all the formal functions of national parliaments in relation to EU affairs.[141] These comprise being kept informed by the EU institutions, verifying respect for subsidiarity, special monitoring of EU activities in justice and home affairs, participation in treaty revision and the enlargement of membership, and in involvement in interparliamentary collaboration.

National parliaments also have explicit powers of assent to changes in decision-making procedures that fall short of treaty revision, mainly involving a shift via a *passerelle* clause from unanimity to QMV or from special to ordinary legislative procedures. There is a general *passerelle* clause which authorises the European Council to change to QMV and co-decision.[142] Specific *passerelles* allow for the adoption of QMV in foreign and security policy, family law, social policy, some reserved items concerning environmental policy and energy supply, the multi-annual financial framework, and enhanced cooperation.[143] Either implicitly or explicitly, deployment of these *passerelle* clauses will require heads of government to get the by-your-leave of national parliaments.

---

[140] Article 10 TEU.
[141] Article 12 TEU.
[142] Article 48(7) TEU.
[143] Respectively, Articles 31(3) TEU and Articles 81(3), 153(2), 192(2), 312(2) and 333 TFEU.

The weakness of national parliaments in dealing with EU affairs to date has been starkly demonstrated by the success of the No votes in France, Holland and Ireland. In those three countries, the fact that almost all the mainstream parliamentary parties of left and right were in favour of Yes proved to have no traction with the electorate. When it comes to Europe, the normal fault lines of national politics seem not to matter.

The Convention was in any case wise to pay heed to the plight of national parliaments in the European dimension, and right to try to enhance parliamentary democracy not only at the European level but also at that of the member state. Two protocols to the treaty address the EU's relationship with national parliaments.[144] In essence, these protocols deal with the matter of the EU's compliance with the principle of subsidiarity in the new constitutional order. National parliaments are invited to assess the scale and effects of draft EU laws in areas of shared or supplementary competence in order to verify that the EU is the right level at which to legislate. Codifying the practice introduced informally by the Barroso Commission, the protocols require the Commission to communicate directly with national parliaments. Parliaments can raise a reasoned objection to a draft law on the grounds of a breach of the principle of subsidiarity.

The subsidiarity test means not only that EU decisions should be taken as close to the citizens as possible, but also that there is proof of added value in reaching the intended objectives at Union level. The objectives of the draft law themselves are not, in the strictest sense, part of the test. Yet national parliamentary scrutiny is bound to bear upon the scope and force of the intended law as made explicit in its drafting, as well as on any likely but unintended consequences. It is important for national parliaments to calculate whether the proposed EU law might be improbably disruptive at the national level, creating disconcerting legal

---

[144] Protocol No. 1 on the role of national Parliaments in the European Union and Protocol No. 2 on the application of the principles of subsidiarity and proportionality.

uncertainty and giving rise to significant potential for judicial conflict.

To help national parliaments, the time allowed for the scrutiny of draft law was raised from six to eight weeks by the Lisbon IGC. Neither the Council nor European Parliament will take a formal position on the draft law until after the expiry of the eight week period.

If, within eight weeks, one third of national parliaments objects the Commission will maintain, amend or withdraw the draft, and give reasons for its decision.[145] This is called, in football parlance, the 'yellow card'. Thereafter, in a further Lisbon revision to the original proposal, if a simple majority of national parliaments continues to object, the Commission will refers their reasoned objection to the Council and Parliament, which will decide there and then whether to end the matter – the 'orange card'.[146] In dealing with an orange card the Council will act abnormally by a 55 per cent majority (without the population factor); Parliament will act by a simple majority.

The Lisbon IGC successfully killed off a silly and dangerous proposal from the Dutch parliament to allow a simple majority of national parliaments to block any legislative initiative. This 'red card' would have pushed national parliaments into direct conflict with the European Parliament, raising the spectre of the development of a third legislative chamber composed of national MPs. Mankind has yet to devise a tricameral legislature, although the EU has had previous experience of a European Parliament made up of delegations of national parliamentarians. In 1979 that system was abolished because it did not work, because MPs had domestic rather than EU mandates, because they could give neither the time nor focus to EU affairs, because they were all elected at different times and for different periods, and, ultimately, because the growing importance of the European

---

[145] Protocol No. 2, Article 7.
[146] Article 7(2) and 7(3) of Protocol No. 2. For the role of national parliaments see also, in particular, Articles 5, 10(2), 12 and 48 (2-3) and (7) TEU and 69, 81 and 352(2) TFEU.

dimension to law and politics demanded a more focussed and professional approach. Given the much greater complexity and sophistication required of EU law makers today than thirty years ago, it defies belief to think that a reincarnation of the old system could work. National parliamentarians have a job to do in the EU, but it is not the job of the MEP, who enjoys a direct popular mandate as EU legislator. It is reactionary nonsense, peddled by the nationalists, to pretend that the collective will of the EU's twenty-seven national parliaments is in some sense a more pure expression of democracy than that of the European Parliament and Council of Ministers acting jointly.

In any case, national parliamentary scrutiny of EU affairs is generally weak and should be improved. Getting the balance right, however, is difficult. There is no one formula that works for twenty-seven different national parliaments. Some parliaments focus on interrogating ministers on their way to and from meetings of the Council; others concentrate on sifting documentation in order to influence government decisions on EU law making; several do next to nothing. Whatever their individual style, all national parliaments meet up within COSAC, the conference of national parliamentary scrutiny committees which exchanges information and best practice. The European Parliament is heavily involved in encouraging interparliamentary collaboration with its national counterparts on a sector by sector basis.

In the workings of the early warning mechanism, the treaty gives two votes to each national parliament in order to meet the constitutional requirements of federal states where, for example, the Bundestag and Bundesrat have distinct roles to play. The Convention's assumption was, however, that in states with bicameral parliaments the two votes would be exercised as one.

Within the same eight weeks as they are reaching their own reasoned opinion, national parliaments will also be minded to coordinate their approach with other national parliaments if the quorum of one third is ever to be reached. The Convention intended that the reasoned opinions should be either identical or at least similar in order to trigger the constitutional early warning mechanism. It was fully aware that in circumstances where one parliament (say the Italian) were to complain that the scale and effects of a draft law did not go far enough, and another parliament (say the British) were to grumble that the same law went too far, the Commission would be perfectly free to ignore them both. Random or contradictory opinions or those that are not reasoned on the grounds of subsidiarity will be a waste of everyone's time.

Each national parliament will have to decide for itself how much effort it wishes to put into this exercise. The treaty does not, indeed cannot, oblige national parliaments to react formally to each piece of draft legislation. In the governance of the European Union, failure to act is the default option. It will not be dishonourable to choose not to intervene. In fact, one suspects that the issuing of formal reasoned opinions from all twenty-seven national parliaments will be very rare.

The early warning mechanism will work none the worse for being deployed infrequently and with discretion. National parliaments would be advised not to be preoccupied with waving the orange card to the exclusion of the more political scrutiny of EU affairs. For example, the multi-annual work programme, the legislative programme, the budgetary settlements, the annual report on comitology, Green and White Papers, and developments in the field of foreign, security and defence policy are all central features of the contemporary EU, equally deserving of scrutiny by national parliaments. National parliaments would do well to pay particular attention to the Commission's annual report on the application of subsidiarity.

The Lisbon treaty succeeds in balancing an enhanced role for national parliaments with respect for the role of the EU legislator. Each EU institution is duty bound to respect the principle of subsidiarity, and not just national parliaments. MEPs and ministers together are responsible for deciding whether a draft law from the Commission is good, bad or

71

indifferent. All three institutions consult widely about draft legislation and are susceptible to lobbying.

The role of national parliaments is both a real one and is genuinely respected, but it is different from that of the EU legislator itself, to whom the duty of law making falls. Their principal function is to sustain and hold to account the government of the day.

The real significance of the early warning mechanism is not that it will be much used, but that it lends itself to the development of good governance in the EU by stimulating informed parliamentary scrutiny of EU affairs in general. The true objective, after all, is to improve the quality of EU public policy. National parliaments can make a significant contribution to achieving this goal by helping the EU institutions to monitor the effect of EU law once in place, by reflecting more regularly and politically upon the European integration process, and by working as a conduit between the federal institutions on the one hand and domestic media and public opinion on the other.

CHAPTER FIVE   PAYING FOR THE UNION

How to deal with the Union's budget played a large part in the constitutional negotiations, but the end product does not depart radically from the current situation. There was no agreement to inject an element of fiscal federalism into the financial system which would have given the EU a serious role in macroeconomic stabilisation policy. The sums available to be spent at EU level will still stand, under Lisbon, at about 2.5 per cent of all public spending. The ceiling on EU revenue remains at 1.24 per cent of the Union's GNI. The EU budget is not allowed to go into deficit. The total size of the annual budget in 2009 is € 116 billion, which amounts to 0.894 per cent of GNI.

So the curious constitutional imbalance remains between the Union's small financial clout on the one hand and its large political and legislative powers on the other. The questions surrounding the future financing of the EU are not so much about redistributing resources between member states but more about maximising the impact of EU common policies so that the added value of every euro spent at European level is enhanced.

Since 1988 an inter-institutional agreement has set a medium-term 'financial perspective' that determines overall planned expenditure and assigns sums to various broad categories. The current period lasts from 2007 until 2013.

Just under 40 per cent of the EU budget is spent on direct support for the agricultural sector mainly by subsidising farmers' incomes and by countryside management schemes. The rest is spent through structural and cohesion funds, particularly in order to stimulate economic activity in the poorer regions as well as infrastructural development, on R&D and on administration.

The new treaty puts a welcome emphasis on the importance of achieving sound financial management.[147] A new law will lay down the control and audit obligations of member states which should provide the Commission with greater powers to enforce compliance.[148] The three institutions will have to pay greater heed to the advice of the Court of Auditors and to be more accountable to each other if the EU budget is to be properly managed at the EU level, faithfully implemented at the national level, and correctly discharged. The Commission has made good progress in smartening up its own accounting procedure. Yet there is an important trade-off to be made between demands for decentralised management and the desire for greater budgetary control. As by far the largest part of the EU budget is spent by national governments, the European Parliament and Commission are encouraging national governments to deliver their own annual statements of assurance about their EU spending – so far, without much success. The public accounts committees of national parliaments might show more of an interest in how EU money is spent.

As far as the EU's 'own resources' are concerned, the treaty sticks to the current system whereby the revenue ceiling and the categories of revenue source are decided by the Council, requiring unanimity, with Parliament only consulted. The agreement then has to be ratified by all national parliaments.

It was agreed within the Convention that the process of setting the financial perspectives, now subject to a voluntary inter-institutional agreement, should be integrated formally into the treaty and that the agreed financial plan – restyled as the 'multi-annual financial framework' – should become obligatory upon the budgetary authority (Council and Parliament).

There was a fierce argument about whether the Council should be able to act by QMV in setting the multi-annual

---

[147] Article 310(5) and(6) TFEU.
[148] Article 317 TFEU.

financial framework. (Parliament has the power of consent.) Here, however, the negotiations stumbled across hard politics. France, Spain and Ireland were determined to protect the bulk of CAP spending from any attack by the British, Dutch and Scandinavians. The Dutch, for their part, linked their grudge against the UK rebate to the financial perspectives: if the British insisted on a veto over EU revenue, the Dutch would insist on a veto on EU spending. The Lisbon treaty, therefore, retains unanimity for the financial perspectives, but permits the European Council, acting unanimously, to switch to QMV at an unspecified future date.[149] This is a prominent example of the use of the device of the *passerelle*, or bridging clause, which introduces the potential for future flexibility.

The present budgetary procedure, which dates from 1975, is complicated. There are different procedures for 'compulsory' and 'non-compulsory' sectors. Parliament is prevented from exercising its full budgetary authority over the compulsory segment, which includes the CAP. Overall, however, Parliament has the power to reject the budget at its third reading by a two-thirds majority. The Council uses QMV to amend Parliament's first reading. To confirm its adherence to its original modifications, Parliament needs a three-fifths majority at its second reading. If no budget can be agreed at all, the previous annual budget is voted through on a monthly basis.

Happily, the Lisbon treaty will succeed in making some big changes to the budgetary procedure by borrowing elements from the tried and tested co-decision procedure used for ordinary legislation. Importantly, the arcane distinction between compulsory and non-compulsory expenditure is abolished. Parliament will have uniform powers over the whole annual budget, including the CAP and the anomalous stand-alone European Development Fund. And the ordinary legislative procedure is to be used to enact

---

[149] Article 312 TFEU.

the financial regulations under which money is actually disbursed and accounted for.[150]

The new budgetary procedure, which is governed by strict timetables, is as follows.[151] Having received the Commission's draft budget, the Council will act in the first instance by QMV. Parliament can then table amendments by an absolute majority or the budget shall stand adopted. Council will accept Parliament's amendments by QMV or reject them and convene a conciliation committee. The conciliation committee's position will stand if either Council or Parliament fails to act. If Parliament accepts the compromise position (by simple majority) but Council rejects it (by QMV), the compromise still stands unless Parliament musters a three-fifths majority to re-impose its first reading amendments. In a rather surreal final scenario, provision is also made for the compromise to be rejected outright by Parliament (acting by absolute majority) or by Council (by QMV) if Parliament fails to act. No matter how the draft budget is defeated, however, the Commission will have to submit a new proposal.

---

[150] Article 322 TFEU.
[151] Article 314 TFEU.

Annual Budgetary Procedure

Article 314 TFEU

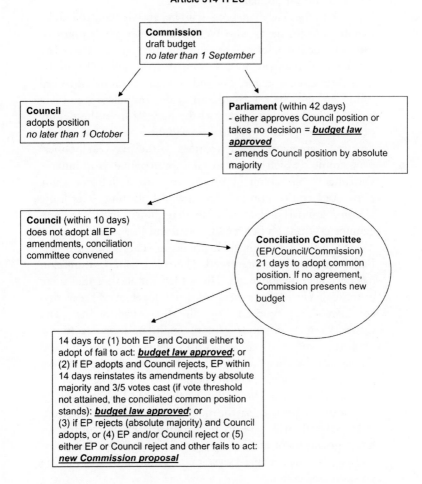

Commission
draft budget
no later than 1 September

Council
adopts position
no later than 1 October

Parliament (within 42 days)
- either approves Council position or takes no decision = ***budget law approved***
- amends Council position by absolute majority

Council (within 10 days) does not adopt all EP amendments, conciliation committee convened

Conciliation Committee (EP/Council/Commission) 21 days to adopt common position. If no agreement, Commission presents new budget

14 days for (1) both EP and Council either to adopt of fail to act: ***budget law approved***; or (2) if EP adopts and Council rejects, EP within 14 days reinstates its amendments by absolute majority and 3/5 votes cast (if vote threshold not attained, the conciliated common position stands): ***budget law approved***; or (3) if EP rejects (absolute majority) and Council adopts, or (4) EP and/or Council reject or (5) either EP or Council reject and other fails to act: ***new Commission proposal***

How are we to assess this complicated tripartite package deal covering the revenue system, medium-term financial planning and the annual budget?

First, the EU's income will be strictly controlled by national governments who will have to win the consent of their respective national parliaments for any change. The European Parliament, in a secondary role, will still only be consulted over revenue. Second, the multi-annual financial framework will be reformed and made compulsory, and will gradually be liberated by dint of the *passerelle* from the rigidity of unanimity. The Commission will be able to propose a financial framework that is married to the five-year political programme which is also its prerogative to initiate. Parliament will exploit its power of consent to force some element of co-decision into the financial planning. Third, the Union's annual budget will be determined by QMV and genuine co-decision between Council and Parliament.

So the states retain their privileges. The standing of the Parliament has been preserved. The role of the Commission has been slightly enhanced. The settlement ensures that there is more likely to be a new annual budget every year that commands the consent of all three institutions. The Commission is set to re-gain the right of initiative in the unlikely event of a stand-off between Council and Parliament, but in practice the final combative phase of the procedure is unlikely to be needed.

Time will tell. The testing of the revised system will be very tough especially as the new financial framework from 2014 onwards will have to be negotiated in the context of heavy government indebtedness in the aftermath of the near collapse of the financial system in 2008 and the ensuing economic recession.

The next review of the EU's own resources should be more radical than the last. Some greater element of fiscal federalism is likely to emerge, driven by the force of logic and fairness. Gross contributions should relate to the ability to pay and spending decisions should accord more faithfully

than they do now to the commonly agreed political priorities
of the Union as a whole.

CHAPTER SIX   THE UNION ABROAD

Only the common foreign, security and defence policies, provided for in the TEU, continue, in the main, to have specifically intergovernmental procedures, usually decided by unanimity.[152] States are required to use these procedures to coordinate their external activities and to define common positions in times of international crisis. Lisbon imposes on EU states strict obligations to consult, to try to reach consensus, but not, in the end, to agree.

With Lisbon, for example, it would be more awkward, although still not impossible, for the UK to invade Iraq in the teeth of opposition from its EU partners. That must be why the UK, in the course of the treaty's renegotiation, sought to add declarations which emphasised the independence of each member state's foreign policy in something of a contradiction to the interdependence implied by the treaty provisions themselves. Yet declarations are of secondary importance to the actual clauses of the treaty: they may have political importance for the future interpretation of the treaty but they do not enjoy the force of law. It must also be recalled that if the UK, for example, sought to assert its sovereign right to unilateral action in contradiction to the spirit of solidarity that underlies the treaty framework for common foreign and security policy, the new treaty will also allow a core group of member states to establish a form of enhanced cooperation in foreign and security policy that would, perforce, exclude the British.

Institutionally speaking, the European Council is to be responsible for determining the strategy and objectives of common foreign and security policy. The Council of Ministers will work within the strategic guidelines established

---

[152] Articles 21-46 TEU.

by the heads of government. Both bodies can take decisions. The common policy will be put into effect by the Vice-President/High Representative and the states themselves, using both national and EU resources.[153] The European Parliament will be regularly consulted on the 'main aspects and basic choices' of the common policy.[154] The Council will act on the basis of a proposal from the Vice-President/High Representative (with or without the Commission's formal support), or from a state.

Security and defence policy

The new treaty puts great emphasis on building an operational capacity in security and defence policy that combines both civilian and military assets. The task is the progressive framing of a common defence policy which may lead, in time, to a common defence when the European Council and national parliaments so decide. (Ireland and, one presumes, Denmark would have a referendum in such circumstances.) In any case, all states 'undertake progressively to improve their military capabilities'.[155]

The European Defence Agency is established with the tasks of identifying measures to strengthen the industrial and technological base of the defence sector, and to help in the definition of European armaments policy and military capabilities.[156] States may choose whether or not to take part in the activities of the Defence Agency – and Ireland is widely expected to withdraw from it as part of its effort to get a positive popular vote on the treaty as a whole. Established already in 2004, the European Defence Agency is entrenched by Lisbon and has its mandate broadened. It will gradually take over the work of existing intergovernmental

---

[153] Article 24(1) TEU.
[154] Article 36 TEU.
[155] Article 42(3) TEU.
[156] Article 45 TEU.

bodies in the armaments field.[157] It also works closely with the European Commission in its own efforts not only to boost R&D in science and technology relevant to Europe's security but also to open up the arms market to more competition. The treaty still allows states to protect their arms industries from normal single market disciplines for reasons of national security, but the Agency will help the Commission limit the widespread abuse of the EU's general competition and public procurement rules in the defence sector.[158]

The treaty refreshes and up-grades the objectives of European security and defence policy.[159] The new tasks of the Union comprise joint disarmament operations, humanitarian and rescue missions, military advice and assistance projects, conflict prevention and peace-keeping missions, and the deployment of combat forces in crisis management, including peace-making and post-conflict stabilisation.[160] The treaty sensibly provides for a certain group of states to embark upon a particular military mission on behalf of the Union as a whole, where the Council sets the objective, scope and conditions.[161]

In a yet more radical change to the current regime, Lisbon permits militarily capable and politically willing states to go forward to permanent structured cooperation in defence.[162] This is a major improvement on the present treaties, which actually prohibit the emergence of a core group in defence matters. While the neutrality of those states

---

[157] The West European Armaments Group (WEAG) and the Organisation Conjointe de Coopération en matière d'Armement (OCCAR).

[158] Article 346 TFEU.

[159] These had been devised initially in 1992 as the 'Petersberg Tasks', named after the hotel on the Rhine in which the intergovernmental agreement was reached.

[160] Article 43 TEU.

[161] Article 42(5) TEU.

[162] Articles 42(6) and 46 TEU and Protocol No. 10 on permanent structured cooperation.

who are not also members of NATO is respected, the way is opened for all those states which may choose to build European defence capacity to do so under the auspices of the EU. As long ago as 1954 the French National Assembly rejected an earlier treaty to found a European Defence Community. Half a century on, Lisbon sets the ball rolling again. The goal is not to create one European army but to integrate Europe's national armed forces so that they might become more modern, cost effective and militarily capable.

The lifting of the prohibition on enhanced co-operation in security and defence policy is one of the most important reforms envisaged by the treaty. The core group will be established by the Council acting by QMV. Unlike the euro, which all states are expected in the end to join, the defence goals of the Union expressly do not require the eventual participation of all states. The qualifications for participation and obligations of membership are tough. Only members of the core group will admit new members, acting by QMV. Other decisions of the core group are to be taken by unanimity. Members of the group are bound in practice to maintain a high level of defence expenditure: at present, only France and the UK spend as much as 2 per cent of their GDP on defence. They are committed to harmonising the identification of military needs by pooling and specialising their defence means and capabilities. They are obliged to take concrete measures to enhance their capacity to deploy fighting troops by making good perceived shortfalls in meeting agreed troop, equipment and logistics commitments.[163] They will harmonise their procurement policies, co-ordinate their training, standardise their equipment and identify common objectives. Any state which no longer fulfils the criteria or is no longer able to meet its commitments will be in danger of being ousted from the core group, also by QMV.[164]

One concrete conclusion of the rise of EU security and defence policy is the effective absorption into the EU of the

---

[163] Article 2 of Protocol No. 10.
[164] Article 46(4) TEU.

Western European Union, which had been founded after the European Defence Community floundered.[165] Because its achievements have been modest throughout its fifty year history, the passing of WEU will not be much lamented, but its erstwhile parliamentary assembly usefully collected together the defence specialists from national parliaments, and these same MPs must now learn to collaborate closely with their counterparts in the European Parliament.

Completing the EU's takeover of WEU, Lisbon introduces a new mutual assistance clause which means that states will be obliged to come to the aid of each other in the event of armed aggression. Commitments under this provision are without prejudice to the status of the neutral states and they will be consistent with NATO obligations 'which, for those States which are members of it, remains the foundation of their collective defence and the forum for its implementation'.[166]

To put its emerging military effort into a clearer political context, in December 2003 the European Council adopted the Union's first European Security Strategy. Formulated by Javier Solana, *A Secure Europe in a Better World* does not mince its words on Europe's military weakness. Its objectives are to tackle the threats to Europe's security, to extend the scope of security around Europe's borders and to strengthen the international order. The document asserts that the main security threats of weapons of mass destruction and terrorism can only be met by 'effective multilateralism'. The EU, it says, will uphold the UN. It remains committed to the use of force only as a last resort. In contrast to the then current American policy of making pre-emptive strikes against potential foes, the EU speaks of 'preventive engagement'. In December 2008 the European Security Strategy was reviewed, alas almost in private.[167] New security risks were identified, including cyber security, energy security, competition for

---

[165] Protocol No. 11 on Article 42 TEU.

[166] Article 42(7) TEU.

[167] See the Presidency Conclusions of the European Council, 11-12 December 2008.

natural resources, security in space and piracy. Russia's new assertiveness sharpened the appreciation of the EU leaders about unresolved disputes in the neighbouring regions.

To date there have been twenty-two ESDP missions, sixteen of them including an important civilian component. The results have been mixed, but useful conclusions can be drawn from this early experience – notably, that there is a need for an EU operational headquarters from which to run these missions. It is also clear that much closer collaboration with NATO is an essential requirement. Coincident to the revival of European security and defence policy was the 60th anniversary summit of NATO and the French decision, under President Sarkozy, to reintegrate its military inside NATO. Not before time the EU is now obliged to fashion a coherent policy towards NATO, not least because of the embarrassment caused by the ambivalent European contribution to the NATO campaign in Afghanistan. The headline goal of European security and defence policy is to make a force of 60,000 fighting troops permanently available for rapid deployment. It is a tall order.

Not least among the security preoccupations of the European Parliament is arms control. The EU Code of Conduct on arms exports is proving to be insufficiently rigorous in controlling unethical commercial practices or in combating illegal arms trafficking. Parliament is demanding binding EU rules on arms brokering, as well as a drive by the EU to achieve an international arms trade treaty. It is to be hoped that best practice in the field of arms procurement engendered by the European Defence Agency will spill over into European arms exportation. An arms control policy grounded within the evolving European Security Strategy, coupled with the revised institutions and procedures promised by the treaty, would indeed give Europe the chance to do good in the world.

Foreign and security policy

In addition to the extension of collective responsibility among the states in the field of defence, the new treaty also contains a solidarity clause which provides for the states to act jointly in the face of a terrorist attack or a natural or man-made disaster.[168] These new provisions should be read as meaning that, although Ireland retains the discretion not to send fighting troops to defend the Baltic states against a Russian invasion, Ireland would be required to respond to requests from a fellow member state for assistance in terms of transportation, medical services or bomb disposal expertise, for example, in the event of a terrorist outrage such as we have seen in Madrid and London – and, indeed, in Northern Ireland.

The Lisbon treaty takes over from the Treaty of Amsterdam (1997) a useful instrument which loosens the straitjacket of unanimity in foreign and security policy: the device of constructive abstention. Short of wielding the national veto against a policy of which it disapproves, a state will be able to allow a decision to be taken but at the same time announce that it will not be bound to apply it itself. This has already proven to be a useful practice in the case of the recognition of the independence of Kosovo.

In a further improvement, the new treaty adds the proviso that all actions taken within European security and defence policy must comply with the principles of the Charter of the United Nations.[169] This makes it crystal clear, not least to the Irish, that the EU gives primacy to the UN – as indeed it is required to do under Article 103 of the UN Charter.

Just as the new treaty opens up the prospect of more variable geometry within the Union, it provides for newly flexible forms of relationship with immediate neighbours. The Union looks to develop a special relationship with neighbouring countries, characterised by co-operation rather than integration. Specific agreements with the countries concerned may contain reciprocal rights and obligations as well as the possibility of undertaking activities jointly.

---

[168] Article 222 TFEU and Declaration 37.
[169] Article 21 TEU.

The EU has considerable experience of co-operation agreements with countries in its immediate environs. The Barcelona Process, established in 1995, embraces almost all the Mediterranean countries in a dialogue with the EU. This was developed in 2008, under the French presidency, into a Union for the Mediterranean. After the break-up of the USSR, several Partnership and Co-operation Agreements were signed with Eastern European states. However, both to the South and to the East the EU's search for effectively reciprocal rights and obligations is still proving elusive.

The challenge for EU member states and the institutions, naturally, is not to work together in foreign affairs when everyone agrees with each other, but to do so despite disagreements. To facilitate the political process, the aims of the Union's international policies are spelled out in detail.[170]

To facilitate the institutional process, Lisbon provides for the use of QMV in four specific cases: when the Council adopts decisions on the basis of a strategic decision of the European Council; when it adopts a decision proposed by the High Representative working under a mandate from the European Council either at his instigation or theirs; when implementing a decision defining a Union action or position; and when appointing a special representative.[171] As the High Representative is in any case empowered to make proposals to the European Council, the flexibility of the decision-making arrangements is really rather large, and the potential scope of QMV broad – in spite of the fact that decisions in the military or defence field are excluded. To prevent too wide a use of QMV, the British insisted on the insertion of the back-stop provision whereby any one state will be able to refer a whole issue to the European Council for a unanimous decision. Yet it should not be forgotten that, as we have noted earlier, the treaty also includes a *passerelle* clause which will enable the European Council in future to widen further the scope of QMV.

---

[170] Article 21 TEU.
[171] Article 31(2) TEU.

States are duty bound to cooperate with each other in third countries and within international organisations. In particular, states which are members of the UN Security Council are supposed to defend the positions and the interests of the Union. The Vice-President/High Representative can be asked to represent the Union at the UN.[172]

External Action Service

In the conduct of the Union's international relations, the creation of the External Action Service, drawing expertise and resources from the states, the Council secretariat and the Commission, is of great significance. Run by the Vice-President/High Representative, the new service will be able to pool intelligence, develop joint analysis and planning capabilities, and speak for the Union with a single voice. The first effects of the External Action Service will be felt by third countries and international organisations whose relations with the EU will become simpler and more straightforward.

The actual establishment of the External Action Service will scarcely be without teething troubles, as the institutions and national foreign ministries view with each other for influence. But it should be possible with skill and good will to develop the new joint service in a way that protects the prerogatives of the Commission and Parliament, engages national diplomacies and provides the Vice-President/High Representative with the resources, intelligence and instruments he will need to function well. Parliament is to be formally consulted about the setting up of the Action Service. (And in a not insignificant addition to Parliament's powers, the ordinary legislative procedure is henceforth to be used for the EU's staff regulation.)[173]

The administrative expenditure of the institutions, mainly the costs of running the External Action Service, is to be charged to the EU budget. The costs of operations will

---

[172] Article 34(2) TEU.
[173] Article 298 TFEU.

also be a call on the EU budget with the exception of military matters, in which case the Council will allocate costs on a case by case basis according to a state's GNI. States who abstain from a decision will not be liable to pay for its consequences. National contributions will finance a start-up fund, to be established by the Council acting by QMV, to pay for the early phase of activities not charged to the EU budget. These financing arrangements are both timid and unnecessarily complicated.[174]

Commercial policy

The basis of the Union's common commercial policy is its customs union, established by the Treaty of Rome. The Lisbon treaty adds the liberalisation of foreign direct investment to the existing goals of commercial policy, which are the harmonious development of world trade, the progressive abolition of restrictions on international trade, and the lowering of customs and other barriers.[175] The new treaty also adds trade in services, intellectual property rights, and foreign direct investment to the definition of the exclusive competence of the commercial policy. The ordinary legislative procedure defines the framework of the common commercial policy.

For international trade agreements, the Council authorises the Commission to open negotiations on the basis of the Commission's recommendations. The Commission is assisted by a special committee made up of national representatives appointed by the Council. The Commission reports to the committee and to Parliament. Council acts by QMV to open and close the negotiations – except in the field of trade in services, intellectual property and foreign direct investment where it acts unanimously if the Union's internal rules require it to do so. At the insistence mainly of France (worried about French), the IGC agreed that Council will also act by unanimity in relation to trade in cultural and audio-visual services where the agreements 'risk prejudicing the

---

[174] Article 41 TEU.
[175] Article 206 TFEU.

Union's cultural and linguistic diversity', and in the case of trade in social, education and health services where the agreements 'risk seriously disturbing the national organisation of such services and prejudicing the responsibility of Member States to deliver them'.[176]

The practice for the negotiation of other international treaties is more or less the same as for trade treaties. For foreign and security policy negotiations, the High Representative can submit recommendations to the Council for the opening of the proceedings. The Council shall nominate him or the Commission to carry out the negotiating mandate. Council needs the consent of Parliament to conclude agreements in the following cases: association agreements; accession to the ECHR; agreements establishing a specific institutional framework by organising co-operation procedures; agreements with important budgetary implications for the Union; agreements covering fields to which either the ordinary legislative procedure applies, or the special legislative procedure where consent by Parliament is required. In all other cases, Parliament will be consulted, often within a set time-limit.

Where issues arise that concern a mixed competence of both common foreign and security policy (under the Treaty on European Union) and the external relations of other common policies (under the Treaty on the Functioning of the European Union), it is the preponderant competence that will determine the legal base.

The whole package on how to regulate the Union's external relations represents a very considerable enhancement of the Parliament's powers not only over the exclusive competence of commercial policy but also in the less charted waters of freedom, security and justice. MEPs can be expected to police their new prerogatives with some attention. Under the current treaties, Parliament has the right of assent only over association agreements or those with important budgetary implications.[177]

---

[176] Article 207(4) TFEU.
[177] Article 300(3) TEC.

The Commission's mandate can be varied, or an international agreement suspended at any stage. A state or any of the institutions may obtain an opinion of the Court of Justice about the compatibility of the agreement with the treaty. In the field of intellectual property rights the powers of the Court are restricted, and any expansion of the Court's powers into IPR will have to be agreed and ratified unanimously.[178] Special arrangements are provided for international agreements concerning the exchange rate of the euro.[179]

Development policy

The primary purpose of the Union's overseas development policy is the reduction and eventual eradication of poverty.[180] For the first time, the budget of the European Development Fund is to be incorporated into the general EU budget, thereby further extending European Parliamentary control. The Commission can take initiatives to ensure the close co-ordination of EU policy with national policies and aid programmes. Similar EU legislation governs economic, financial and technical co-operation with third countries and the EU's disaster relief work. The Union's humanitarian aid operations are to be conducted in compliance with the principles of international law: impartial, neutral and non-discriminatory.[181] The treaty provides for the setting up of a new voluntary humanitarian aid corps for young Europeans.

Provision is made for the imposition of economic and financial sanctions against one or more third countries, natural or legal persons or non-state entities, like Al-Qaida.[182] The Council shall act by QMV on a joint proposal of the Vice-President/High Representative and Commission. Parliament will be informed.

---

[178] Article 262 TFEU.
[179] Article 219 TFEU.
[180] Article 208 TFEU.
[181] Article 214(2) TFEU.
[182] Article 215(2) TFEU.

Complicated as all these institutional arrangements may seem, the Lisbon treaty provides mechanisms for bringing the international profile of the European Union into much sharper perspective. For the rest of the world, Europe will be easier to deal with if and when the proposals of the treaty are implemented. Everyone will benefit from the focus brought by Lisbon to defining the Union's objectives in foreign, security and defence policy as well as in commercial policy and overseas aid and development. The institutional provisions of the treaty are the basis for changing the dynamics of Europe's external activities. The Vice-President/High Representative will be a powerful person. Much will depend on his or her ability to suppress old jealousies and divisions between Commission, Council and European Council as well as among the national diplomacies of the states. There is little doubt that Europe needs this additional capability if it is to act effectively on the world stage. The troubled borders of the European Union in the Caucasus and the Middle East make such an advance indispensable to its own security interests.

CHAPTER SEVEN   FREEDOM, SECURITY AND JUSTICE

The acquisition by the Union of a single legal personality in international law means, among other things, that the 'third pillar' in the field of justice and home affairs, invented at Maastricht, will disappear entirely. Lisbon allows a five year transition period. Common policies in the area of freedom, security and justice, including the Schengen agreement which effectively creates a passport union, are to be assimilated within the old 'first pillar'. Here they will be accorded the full treatment of the classic Community method, invented for customs, economic and social affairs, whereby the Commission proposes and the Council and Parliament dispose, all under the watchful supervision of the Court of Justice. The Commission will also gain the power to launch infringement procedures against states which refuse to implement EU law – a significant reform in the area of police and judicial cooperation in criminal justice where the old system of Maastricht simply has not worked.

In this policy sector the Commission will have to share its right to initiate legislation with a group of states numbering at least one quarter of the size of the total membership.[183] However, this is still a significant improvement on the present arrangements, introduced by the Treaty of Amsterdam, whereby any single state can initiate a proposal. The freedom of member states to make unilateral proposals in justice and home affairs has been proved to be, as many predicted, an almost entirely fruitless derogation from the normal method of law making in the Union in which the Commission has the unique authority to seek out and formulate the common interests of all states.

So the reforms of Lisbon are essential if the EU is to make progress in combating crime and ensuring sound

---

[183] Article 76 TFEU.

justice. This is recognised in theory even by those states which retain reservations about the loss of national control over these traditional areas of sovereign autonomy. It will take time for the Union to establish solid trust between the states about crime and justice matters. As a recognition of this lingering apprehension, certain 'emergency brakes' are inserted into the Lisbon provisions which allow any state *in extremis* to appeal to the European Council were it to conclude that a vital national interest was at stake. In all those cases, however, in a neat counterpoint, other states would be automatically propelled forward into a form of enhanced cooperation, leaving the reluctant one or ones behind.

Mindful of the deteriorating internal security situation in the Union, the Convention and subsequent IGCs were determined to enlarge the Union's competences in relevant fields. The new area of freedom, security and justice aims to promote mutual confidence between the competent national authorities on the basis of mutual recognition of judicial and extrajudicial decisions, and to establish operational co-operation between the police and customs.[184]

There is no reluctance on the side of national police and customs officers to collaborating with each other – rather the contrary. In the judicial area, however, more systematic coordination is required: hence the emphasis in the Lisbon treaty on mutual recognition in the field of criminal justice. National parliaments are given the option of participating expressly in the evaluation of the principle of mutual recognition.[185] Representatives of national parliaments appear in general to support the cautious approach adopted by their governments. Given the complexity and sensitivity of EU involvement in justice and home affairs, it is a remarkable achievement of the new treaty that it manages to broaden the scope and objectives of common policy in this area.

The purpose of the Union's area of freedom, security and justice is to remove internal border controls and, accordingly, to frame a common policy on asylum,

---

[184] Article 67 TFEU.
[185] Article 70 TFEU.

immigration and external border control. Immigration policy is intended to be based on solidarity between the different states as well as being fair towards third-country nationals. The EU is empowered to take measures to combat crime, racism and xenophobia, and to impel the collaboration of police and judicial authorities. Judgments in national civil and criminal courts are to be recognised mutually by all states, and criminal laws will be approximated where necessary.

The Lisbon treaty provides for EU legislation on visas, border checks, conditions under which third-country nationals may travel within the EU, and the management of external borders.[186] It creates a general legal base for a comprehensive system for asylum and refugees with uniform standards and common procedures. Such a system will respect the Geneva Conventions on the status of refugees, but may offer higher protection. EU law may establish a uniform status for asylum seekers and those who seek subsidiary protection, a common system for dealing with a temporary massive influx of refugees, common procedures for granting and withdrawing asylum status, criteria and mechanisms for determining which state is responsible for each asylum case, common reception standards, and the conduct of co-operation with third countries. In migration emergencies the Council adopts regulations or decisions on a proposal from the Commission, after consulting the Parliament.[187]

With respect to immigration, and the 'efficient management of migration flows', EU legislation will define the conditions of entry and residence and the rights of third-country legal residents. EU laws will address illegal immigration, including repatriation, and the trafficking of women and children. The EU may adopt incentive measures for the integration of legal immigrants, such as the 'blue card' scheme.[188] EU common policy will not affect the right of states to determine the volume of immigrants they wish to

---

[186] Article 77 TFEU.
[187] Article 78(3) TFEU.
[188] Article 79 TFEU.

accept, although they will be expected to pay their fair share.[189] Asylum and immigration policy will no longer be purely national.

The Treaty of Amsterdam ordained that after a transitional period of five years QMV could be used in the Council to legislate on policies concerning border controls, visas, third country residence, asylum seekers, refugees and immigration.[190] In January 2005, indeed, QMV was eventually introduced for all these questions except that of legal immigration. Lisbon codifies this welcome reform, as well as lifting previous restrictions on the scope of the Court of Justice in this area.

The treaty allows for the integration of civil law with cross-border implications.[191] EU legislation in this field may provide for mutual recognition and enforcement, exchange of documentation, compatibility of jurisdictions, co-operation in taking evidence, access to justice, elimination of obstacles to civil proceedings, alternative methods of dispute settlement, and training of the judiciary. Although the ordinary legislative procedure applies for normal civil matters, special Council measures, with ministers acting unanimously and Parliament only consulted, is retained for family law questions; and any national parliament can veto a draft measure in family law.

Criminal law

Equally sensitive, if not more so, is the potential accorded the European Union under the treaty to make incursions into judicial co-operation in criminal matters. EU measures which may seem perfectly acceptable to deal with cross-border crime can easily impinge upon national courts in their treatment of purely domestic crime over questions such as the admissibility of evidence, the scope of criminal liability, the rights of victims, the weight of penalty or the choice of jurisdiction. EU legislation is foreseen in relation to rules for

---

[189] Article 80 TFEU.
[190] Article 67(2) TEC.
[191] Article 81 TFEU.

mutual recognition of judgments, avoidance and settlement of conflicts between jurisdictions, training of the judiciary, and systems of co-operation. Minimum rules may be established.

Progress on these matters under the existing Treaty of Nice has been minimal. Between 2002 and 2008 ten instruments in mutual recognition have been adopted in Council. However, only one, the European Arrest Warrant, has been implemented by all the states. The Commission and Parliament have been highly critical of the lack of discipline among states in transposing these EU criminal law measures into domestic legislation.

In the field of criminal law, the UK, in particular, insisted on the inclusion of a provision that allows any one state to object to the use of the ordinary legislative procedure on the grounds that 'fundamental aspects of its criminal justice system' would be affected by the draft law.[192] That being the case, the matter will have to be referred to the European Council, which has four months in which it must either terminate the suspension or request a new draft law. If no action is taken or a new draft law is held up for twelve months, and at least one third of member states wish to adopt the law, they shall be permitted to do so. So there is not only an emergency brake to stop progress by the whole Union but an emergency throttle to accelerate the formation of a core group of integrationist member states so that they might proceed without hindrance.

The new treaty also authorises EU law making to establish minimum rules to combat serious crime with cross-border implications in the following areas: terrorism, trafficking in human beings and sexual exploitation of women and children, illicit drug trafficking, illicit arms trafficking, money laundering, corruption, counterfeiting of means of payment, computer crime and organised crime. Those areas may be extended unilaterally by the Council, acting unanimously after consulting the Parliament. In this

---

[192] Article 82(3) TFEU.

field too, the same emergency brake and throttle procedure is prescribed.[193] Special arrangements will be put in place, according to the ordinary legislative procedure, to counter fraud against the financial interests of the Union.[194]

Eurojust, established by a Council decision in 2002, is the network of national prosecution authorities. The powers of Eurojust are widened under the treaty to embrace the investigation and not just prosecution authorities, and also to oblige states to launch a prosecution. EU laws are to determine the structure, operation, scope and tasks of Eurojust. They will also make arrangements for European and national parliamentary scrutiny of Eurojust.[195] The powers of Eurojust may be extended by a unilateral decision of the European Council, acting unanimously, after obtaining the consent of Parliament and after consulting the Commission. Furthermore, the Council, acting unanimously with the consent of Parliament, could establish the office of European Public Prosecutor – and probably will do so once there has been more experience of working within an EU level network of national prosecutors.[196]

The treaty also allows the EU to legislate to develop co-operation between national police forces, including the exchange and storage of data, staff training, research into crime, and the detection of organised crime. The Council alone may legislate, acting unanimously after consulting the Parliament, in the matter of police operations and the involvement of Eurojust and Europol in the internal affairs of states.[197]

Europol is the European Police Office established by a convention in 1995. It collects, analyses and exchanges information among national police authorities. Lisbon gives it a similar legal base to that of Eurojust.[198] Europol and

---

[193] Article 83(3) TFEU.
[194] Article 325 TFEU.
[195] Article 85(1) TFEU.
[196] Article 86 TFEU.
[197] Articles 87 and 89 TFEU.
[198] Article 88 TFEU.

Eurojust exchange information on personal data with each other. Both are destined to develop into more recognisable federal agencies with more powers, a higher profile and a consequent need for greater parliamentary accountability.

The sensitivity of various states in agreeing to the incorporation of justice and home affairs within the competences of the EU and the powers of its institutions was evident in their supreme hesitation in extending the powers of the Court of Justice in this field. The Court is to have no jurisdiction to review the validity or proportionality of operations carried out by the national police or security services, nor to review national arrangements for the maintenance of law and order and the safeguarding of internal security.[199] Lisbon is, nevertheless, an improvement on Nice in this regard: under the current treaty, states have to choose positively to opt into the Court's jurisdiction.[200] The new treaty, by contrast, will enable national courts automatically to refer to the European Court of Justice on all justice and home affairs matters, including asylum and immigration, except for police and security service operations – and except for British and Irish courts in those specific areas where their governments have opted out.[201]

Europe on the move

Of course, people do not have to turn to crime to experience the full force of the Union's emerging area of freedom, security and justice. Following the end of the Cold War there has been a huge churning of Europe's population as people, especially the young, move from city to city in search of fortune. Equally, there are many older people, especially from the gloomy North, who move to sunnier parts to enjoy a second or retirement home. Modern transport and communications mean that living abroad is not

---

[199] Article 276 TFEU.

[200] Article 35(2) TEU (Nice).

[201] Article 2 of Protocol No. 21 on the position of the United Kingdom and Ireland in respect of the area of freedom, security and justice.

the isolating experience that it once may have been. Buying goods and services on the internet is seldom an exclusively national business. The definition of what is a purely 'British job' defies even the most militant trade unionist. Cheap flights make tourism a massive industry. Football fans travel happily across Europe to watch their clubs win or lose. And the euro makes transactions uncomplicated. Students think it natural to take a second degree in a country other than their own. But language learning has spread well beyond the educated élites. More and more are marrying, having children and divorcing by, with and from partners of a different European nationality.

Finally Europe is on the move again. All these phenomena are the products of an integration process that was started and is sustained by the law and politics of the European Union. All these European people need a reliable framework in which to live and move and have their being. The Treaty of Lisbon provides it. It also provides the incentive to respect and promote fundamental rights across Europe, as well as the ways and means to lift standards of civil and judicial administration in the continuing battle against corruption.

CHAPTER EIGHT   CORE GROUPS AND THE REST

One of the great advances of the Lisbon treaty is that it will make it both more easy and more purposeful for a core group of states to decide to go further and faster in the direction of integration in any given policy sector.[202] Put simply, a group of nine or more states may choose to use QMV in cases where unanimity will still apply in the Council of twenty seven.[203]

The concept of enhanced co-operation among a group of states is often confused with a mere 'multi-speed Europe' in which states arrive at commonly agreed destination in their own time. It is perfectly natural that different states converge at different speeds on objectives that are established by the Union as a whole. The gradual and steady expansion of the membership of the Union – peppered as enlargement is with transition periods and temporary derogations – is itself one example of a multi-speed Europe. The same approach has been adopted for the euro: in theory, at least, every EU state is supposed to adopt the single currency as and when it meets the convergence criteria.

By enhanced co-operation, however, the Union means something rather different and a lot more flexible. It was first introduced in a limited way and as a last resort by the Treaty of Amsterdam. Although the states in the core group have to respect a general provision that their action is designed to protect the interests of the Union and to further the integration process as a whole, it is clear that their choice of policy objectives might be very different to those states which either choose to stay outside the core group or, for one reason or another, are obliged to remain outside. Once established, the inner circle could adopt policies that are

---

[202] Article 20 TEU.
[203] Articles 330 and 333 TFEU.

divergent from those still pursued by the outer circle. Although it is to be hoped that any core group would succeed over time in recruiting more members, such inclusiveness cannot be guaranteed. In theory, a core group works as a motor of integration, showing the way forward to all by example. In practice, however, once out in front the self-selected core group could swiftly become a co-opting and self-serving club of the élite, creating perforce not a Europe of multi-speeds but of multi-tiers. In other words, a core group formed under the treaty's provisions of enhanced co-operation may not be a temporary, but a permanent phenomenon.

Enhanced cooperation, as we have already noted, is prohibited in the areas of exclusive competence. Lisbon lowered the threshold to nine states. Enhanced co-operation must not undermine the single market by creating barriers to trade or distorting competition; nor must it undermine the economic, social and territorial cohesion of the Union.[204] The core group must respect the competences, rights and obligations of non-participating states, but, conversely, the outsiders shall not impede the implementation of enhanced co-operation.[205]

The rules covering the authorisation of enhanced co-operation were relaxed somewhat by the Treaty of Nice and further by Lisbon.[206] States wishing to form a core group will need to address the request to the Commission specifying the scope and objectives of the enhanced co-operation proposed.[207] The Council will act to establish enhanced co-operation by QMV on a favourable proposal of the Commission after having first obtained the consent of the European Parliament. All possibility of a single national veto has been removed by Lisbon. The granting of a comprehensive right of consent to Parliament, which in the

---

[204] Article 326 TFEU.
[205] Article 327 TFEU.
[206] Article 11(2) TEC.
[207] Article 329 TFEU.

previous Treaties was very restricted, is a big breakthrough for MEPs.

By contrast, enhanced co-operation in the field of common foreign and security policy will be authorised by the Council acting unanimously on receipt of the advice of the Vice-President/High Representative and Commission. Parliament will be merely informed.

In all cases apart from military matters, the Commission and the participating states must promote the participation of as many states as possible.[208] Late or additional applications to join the core group will be authorised by the Commission within four months.[209] If the Commission rejects the application it must explain why and propose measures to allow the applicant member state to catch up. If a second application is rejected, the failed candidate may appeal to the Council, in which the participating states only will decide the matter by QMV. In short, the conditions of entry for late arrivals are tough. In foreign and security policy, new admissions will be decided by the Council, acting unanimously among the participating states alone.

In theory, all states may take part in Council deliberations on matters subject to enhanced co-operation, even if it is the participating states alone that will take the decisions.[210] Yet whereas the ministers adhering to the core group are free to run their own affairs in the Council, the new treaty is silent on the role of MEPs, judges and Commissioners coming from non-participating states. The presumption must be that the functioning of these other institutions will not be affected. Members of the Parliament, Court of Justice and the Commission represent the common interests of the Union as a whole and all its citizens, and not just their own constituency, jurisdiction or nationality. Nevertheless, it is naïve to imagine that utilisation of enhanced co-operation will not create certain unfortunate rivalries between the 'ins' and the 'outs'.

---

[208] Article 328(1) TFEU.
[209] Article 331 TFEU.
[210] Article 330 TFEU

The key change introduced by Lisbon is that which empowers the core group to decide, albeit by unanimity but without the interference of non-participating states, to switch the decision-making procedure on any provision of the treaty from unanimity to QMV and from a Council law under an abnormal procedure to the ordinary legislative procedure. This means that the core group, once established, can drop all the atypical acts and by-pass all emergency brakes and appeals to the European Council, and proceed to pass laws in the normal way by QMV plus co-decision with the Parliament on a proposal from the Commission.

The potential is large. A nervous Declaration has been attached to the treaty which says that states may indicate, when making a request to establish enhanced co-operation, if they intend already at that stage to make use of the *passerelle* to QMV.[211] As enhanced co-operation is only likely to be needed in precisely those areas where the existence of unanimity causes intolerable frustration, this is a rather bizarre and even superfluous decoration. The fact is that Lisbon makes it impossible to stop the development of an inner core of nine or more states – presumably members already both of the eurogroup and the Schengen area – from fulfilling more ambitious plans for political union.

The Schengen area

What consequences does the new treaty hold for the Union's existing forms of differentiated integration? The Schengen Agreement is the most striking example of enhanced co-operation in practice. It was achieved by a roundabout route. In 1985 five member states signed a convention outside the EU treaty framework at the Luxembourg village of Schengen.[212] The purpose of this agreement was the gradual abolition of passport checks and customs controls at their own respective borders. Revised in 1990, the Schengen Agreement was then absorbed into the Treaty of Amsterdam by a protocol, and was henceforward

---

[211] Declaration 40 on Article 329 TFEU.
[212] Benelux, France and Germany.

an integral part of the acquis communautaire.[213] Each accession state is obliged to sign the Schengen accord, although its practical application is subject to transitional arrangements. Three non-EU countries are also part of the Schengen area. Iceland and Norway were incorporated on account of their membership of the older Nordic passport union. Switzerland joined after complex negotiations and referendums in 2008.

Denmark is a signatory to Schengen, but has had only a partial engagement ever since it had to renegotiate its terms of EU membership after its negative referendum on Maastricht.[214] Where unanimity is required in the Council for decisions in the area of freedom, security and justice, unanimity is defined as unanimity minus Denmark, and the QMV thresholds are adjusted accordingly. At present, Denmark takes little part in this major Union policy area, with the exception of visa policy. (A similar opt-out applies for Denmark, a NATO member, in relation to defence policy.) Denmark may suppress its Schengen protocol in whole or in part at any time it chooses – and it is hoped that the successful entry into force of the Lisbon treaty will create favourable conditions under which the Danish people, by way of referendums, will indeed agree to jettison their country's opt-outs on Schengen, defence policy and euro membership.

As any European traveller well knows, the UK and Ireland are not signatories of Schengen. Under the current treaties, both countries may elect to opt in to all or some of Schengen's provisions on an ad hoc basis, and both have used this facility to some extent. Britain and Ireland have joined the Schengen information exchange system (SIS) and have adopted much of the Schengen regime on asylum – although not on immigration.

---

[213] Protocol No. 19 on the Schengen *Acquis* integrated into the framework of the EU.
[214] Protocol No. 22 on the position of Denmark.

The British and Irish opt-outs

The UK and, more reluctantly, Ireland have negotiated over the years a number of specific protocols which allow them to either opt into or opt out of EU common policies concerning the area of freedom security and justice. The Lisbon IGC gave them a fresh opportunity to assert their autonomy in relation to Schengen, border checks, asylum and immigration and judicial co-operation in civil and criminal matters.[215] Ireland and the UK also decline to recognise the right of the Union to regulate administrative co-operation between themselves and other states, or to legislate for the gathering of information by police.[216] They will also resist any Court of Justice ruling interpreting these articles. Voting thresholds in the Council are adjusted for these items accordingly. The two have three months after the launching of any measure under these provisions to decide whether or not they wish to join in, but they are unable to form part of any blocking minority. Only Ireland has the right to withdraw unilaterally from this self-imposed semi-detachment: the UK would need to convene an IGC.

The UK opt-outs in the field of justice and home affairs are particularly bizarre given the propensity of the British police forces to participate as fully as possible in as many aspects of integration as the law allows. Despite the political reservations, the UK strongly supports Europol. The Schengen arrangements on finger print recognition have been used by UK immigration officers to send hundreds of asylum seekers back to their original point of entry into the EU. The UK has twice challenged the Schengen countries in the Court of Justice to seek better admittance to the use of Schengen databases and frontier control, both times without success.

In fact, the Lisbon treaty is notable for having toughened up the conditions under which the UK and Ireland enjoy their special terms of engagement. The two

---

[215] Protocol No. 21 on the position of the United Kingdom and Ireland in respect of the area of freedom, security and justice.
[216] Articles 74 and 87(2a) TFEU, respectively.

states may exercise their privileges only in accordance with terms, conditions and timetables to be established in each case by the Council and Commission (who will try to maximise both participation and coherence).[217] The UK and Ireland may not opt in at the beginning of a legislative procedure and, then, at the end, opt out. Nor may they stick with an existing policy if the others wish to revise it. Nor may they pick and choose to take part in some aspects of the Schengen agreement – for example, the information system (SIS) – while refusing to accept closely related obligations, such as the protection of data. Nor may the UK continue to participate in existing common policies if, after a transitional period of five years, it refuses to accept the new powers of the Commission, Parliament or Court.[218] In other words, the UK can escape having an infringement action launched against it by the Commission, but it cannot also enjoy the fruits of the relevant common measure.

In pursuit of yet another British 'red line' in the Lisbon IGC, the UK government obliged its partners to raise the barrier with respect to the free movement of workers. It was conceded that any state may now veto a law on labour mobility by claiming that it affects 'important' (rather than 'fundamental') aspects of its national social security.[219] By pressing another emergency brake, the European Council may suspend the legislative process.

Joining and leaving the Union

The development of the European Union has been fashioned directly not only by the incremental process of treaty change but also by the size of its membership. Lisbon changes both dynamics. Membership is open to all European states that respect its values and are committed to promoting them together. Lisbon strengthened the role of national parliaments in the enlargement process by laying down that national parliaments, in addition to the European Parliament,

---

[217] Article 5 of Protocol No. 19; Protocol 21; Declarations 44-47.
[218] Article 10, Protocol No. 36 on transitional provisions.
[219] Article 48 TFEU.

will have to be notified that an application has been made.[220] The Council will decide to accept or reject membership by unanimity after having received the opinion of the Commission and having obtained the consent of the European Parliament, acting by an absolute majority. The accession agreement is made between all the member states and the candidate country and then ratified by all states according to their constitutional requirements.

With respect to enlargement, the new treaty raises the stakes. The European Council is expected to lay down 'conditions of eligibility' which shall be taken into account. This new injunction refers, first, to the original Copenhagen criteria of 1993 in which the European Council responded to the new horizons opened up by the fall of the Berlin Wall and the collapse of the Soviet bloc. It also refers to the European Council of December 2004 which agreed to open accession negotiations with Croatia and Turkey. At that meeting, the heads of government established a new framework for all future accession negotiations. The process became tougher. Permanent safeguard clauses as well as long transition periods and derogations are in future to be considered, not least for the application in practice of the principle of free movement of persons. In a carefully argued passage, the European Council declared:

> 'The shared objective of the negotiations is accession. The negotiations are an open-ended process, the outcome of which cannot be guaranteed beforehand. While taking account of all Copenhagen criteria, if the candidate state is not in a position to assume in full all the obligations of membership it must be ensured that the candidate state concerned is fully anchored in the European structures through the strongest possible bond.'[221]

---

[220] Article 49 TEU.
[221] European Council Presidency Conclusions, Brussels, 16-17 December 2004, para. 23.

The heads of government also added the possibility of suspending the accession negotiations on the initiative of the Commission or of one third of the states in the case of a serious and persistent breach of the principles on which the Union is founded.[222] The Council will decide on such a suspension by QMV after having given a hearing to the candidate state.

The criteria for suspending accession negotiations are drawn directly from the new treaty which provides for the suspension of actual membership on the basis of 'reasoned initiatives' from one third of member states, the Parliament or the Commission.[223] The Council will determine if there is a clear risk of a serious breach, acting by a specially high qualified majority of four-fifths of its members, after obtaining the consent of Parliament. The matter then passes to the level of heads of government, where the European Council, having obtained the consent of MEPs, may determine, by unanimity (minus the alleged offender), the existence of a 'serious and persistent breach'. The Council, acting again by a super qualified majority, could then suspend certain membership rights, including voting rights, although the offending state would not be released of its EU treaty obligations. Similar procedures are in place to vary or revoke the suspension measures. Parliament acts throughout this procedure by a majority of two-thirds, representing a majority of its component members.

The Lisbon treaty, following the work of the Convention and the 2004 constitutional treaty, takes the very significant step in setting down, for the first time, the conditions which will determine the process whereby a state decides to withdraw voluntarily from the Union.[224] It has always been the case that any member state could leave the Union under the terms of the Vienna Convention on the Law of Treaties by unilaterally revoking its accession agreement. But hitherto no EU treaty has provided for an orderly

[222] Article 2 TEU.
[223] Article 7 TEU.
[224] Article 50 TEU.

secession negotiation designed to preserve as much as possible of good relations between the departing state and its erstwhile partners. Luckily, perhaps, no member state has decided to leave the Union, although the Danish overseas territory of Greenland did so. (And Norway twice declined to accept the offer of membership.) Under Lisbon, however, a country which chose to secede would try to negotiate the framework for its future relationship with the Union. In the event that such a negotiation failed, the EU treaties would cease to apply to the disaffected state two years after it had notified the Council of its withdrawal (unless that period was extended by mutual agreement).

Changing the Union

The Treaty of Lisbon offers three revision procedures: one concerning policy changes, one concerning decision-making procedures, and the third concerning amendment of the treaty itself. All three contain a significant new role for the European Parliament.

The first simplified revision procedure allows the European Council to adopt a unanimous decision to revise all or part of Part Three of the Treaty on the Functioning of the EU relating to the internal policies and action of the Union.[225] Any state, the Commission or the Parliament may initiate this procedure, which, however, may not be used to increase the competences of the Union. The European Council will simply decide on these treaty amendments – dispensing with the cumbersome process of the Intergovernmental Conference – after consulting the Parliament, the Commission and, where appropriate, the European Central Bank. Such fast-track amendments will still need to be ratified by all states according to their own constitutional requirements before entering into force, but the intention is to use national parliaments as opposed to popular referendums.

---

[225] Article 48(6) TEU.

The significance of this reform, which introduces a more flexible treaty amendment procedure for the first time since the Treaty of Paris, should not be missed.[226] In creating a softer mechanism for the revision of EU common policies, the Lisbon treaty establishes a hierarchy between different parts of the Union's constitutional order. It is demonstrably not true, as is sometimes alleged by opponents of the Union, that the new treaty will concretise the present state of the Union for all time. The clear intention of the authors of the reform is to make it easier to amend the treaties in future. It should be very useful instrument as the Union draws conclusions for the future of its economic and monetary union in the wake of the current crisis. (Perhaps more should have been made of this point by the Yes campaigners in France, Holland and Ireland – and less of the durability of the constitutional package.)

The second revision procedure is already more famous.[227] The general *passerelle* or bridging clause first appeared in the Convention's early drafts of the constitution, and has provoked much argument and some misunderstanding. Its purpose is to allow, without the paraphernalia of an IGC, the option of extending QMV and co-decision into provisions where the treaty provides for unanimity in the Council and only a minor role for the Parliament. It is a major and welcome constitutional innovation.

Any proposal by the European Council to deploy the *passerelle* will be notified to national parliaments, any one of whom has six months to object. In the absence of opposition, the European Council may adopt the decision after having obtained the consent of an absolute majority in the European Parliament.

---

[226] Article 95 of the Treaty of Paris (1952) establishing the Coal and Steel Community allowed for minor treaty changes to be made if they secured, following a favourable opinion from the Court of Justice, a majority of three-quarters of the votes cast in the Parliament representing two-thirds of Members.

[227] Article 48(7) TEU.

The third type of revision procedure relates to the more constitutional elements of the treaty, including the Charter of Fundamental Rights, the chapters on citizenship, external action, the institutions, financial system and enhanced cooperation. The 'ordinary revision procedure' keeps the present dual key of unanimity in an IGC plus ratification by all member states.[228]

Yet Lisbon makes five important changes to the ordinary revision procedure. First, it institutionalises the holding of a Convention as the normal way of drafting constitutional amendments in preparation of an IGC. A Convention will not be held only if the European Parliament grants its consent to not holding a Convention (an unlikely eventuality). Second, in another leap forward, Parliament gains the right of initiative to propose treaty amendments, alongside the Commission and the states. This radical reform brings to an end the exclusively intergovernmental character of the Union's constituent process. Parliament's right of initiative coupled with the formal installation of the Convention into the treaty reflects the general acceptance of Parliament's role as a constitutional player.

In the aftermath of the French and Dutch No votes, the Lisbon IGC agreed to add the stipulation that the ordinary revision procedure can be used either to increase or to reduce the competences conferred on the Union by the states.[229]

Another useful clarification concerns the procedure for the opening of the treaty revision process. The decision will be taken by the European Council acting by simple majority, after having consulted the Commission and Parliament.[230] This removes the ambiguity surrounding earlier IGCs: Margaret Thatcher, for example, was frustrated by her inability to veto the convening of the IGCs which, in Milan in 1984 led to the Single European Act, and in Dublin in 1990 led to Maastricht.

---

[228] Article 48(4) TEU.
[229] Article 48(2) TEU.
[230] Article 48(3) TEU.

The last addition to the ordinary revision procedure admits the possibility of a failure to ratify a future amended treaty. If, two years after the signature of a new treaty, four fifths of the states have ratified but one or more states have encountered difficulties in proceeding to ratification, there will be a crisis meeting of the European Council to consider the matter.[231] On the face of it, to call a special meeting of the European Council is hardly a radical constitutional innovation, but its implication is rather clear: no one state (nor even a minority of one fifth of the states) should have an automatic or absolute right to block the constitutional progress desired by the majority.

Federalists unite

In conclusion, with the new treaty in force, the Union will not have to seek the transfer of major new competences from the member states. Although some further rationalisation and simplification will continue to be both possible and desirable, the system of government achieved by Lisbon should, in all essentials, be strong. The basic institutional architecture established by the constitutional Convention has survived intact. Although some of the new treaty's provisions will be more long-lasting than others, a particular sense of accomplishment should be appreciated with respect to the powers of the European Parliament. Unsurprisingly, the Parliament strongly endorsed the Treaty of Lisbon by 525 votes to 115 (with 29 abstentions) on 20 February 2008.[232] But national parliaments too have recognised the great advance that the treaty represents for parliamentary democracy in general: the votes for the treaty in twenty five national parliaments (not excluding the Irish) have been overwhelming. One exception is the British parliament where, in the closest indicative vote on whether to accept the treaty or not, on 11 June 2008, 218 MPs voted in favour of having a referendum (with 280 against).

---

[231] Article 48(5) TEU.
[232] OJ C 96E of 17-04-2008.

The other exception is the Czech parliament where ratification is proving to be a tardy, protracted and painful process. On 18 February 2009 the lower chamber approved the treaty by 125 votes to 61 – five more than needed to cross the threshold of three-fifths. The battle now moves to the Czech senate.

What changes that are made by the Treaty of Lisbon to the earlier constitutional treaty were necessary in order to overcome the obstacles caused by France, Holland and the UK. The changes, which are not all bad, will result in a more differentiated and less uniform kind of integration, particularly for the UK and Ireland, but also Poland with respect to the Charter. Such differentiation is likely to be needed as and when the Union enlarges again to take in the countries of the Western Balkans and eventually other countries, possibly including Turkey. If all the opt outs gained by the states – 'the easing of obligations' – were ever exploited to the full the result would surely be that a core group would form to push European integration forward in the federalist direction, leaving behind a nationalist rump. The goal of the next few years is to make that prospective federal core as large as possible.

CHAPTER NINE   EUROPEAN CITIZENSHIP AND THE INTERNAL MARKET

Europe's political reaction to its acute and largely unforeseen economic problems will be influenced by how the Union conducts itself across the whole spectrum of public policy, with its new powers attributed by the Lisbon treaty and its capacity to act refreshed. The social dimension of European integration is shaped in part by the stresses and strains of economic and monetary union, which we examine in the next chapter, but also by the introduction and subsequent evolution of the concept of European Union citizenship.[233] Few EU citizens feel completely at home in the new large economic society that has been opened up to them by the European Union. Size, distance and competition are worrying concepts. In place of a strong affinity between the EU's many nationalities, there is a sense of us belonging only to a community of fellow-strangers. The gift of new rights and privileges is all very well, but the Union also has to work hard to instil a real sense of solidarity among its citizens.

The highly sensitive nature of European citizenship issues is recognised in the Lisbon treaty by the decision to adopt abnormal procedures designed to manage national sensibilities. Although the ordinary legislative procedure will be used to lay down rules to prohibit discrimination on the grounds of nationality, for EU laws banning discrimination based on sex, race, religion, disability, age or sexual orientation, the Council will act unanimously after obtaining the consent of the Parliament. Only the basic principles behind these measures will be established by QMV and co-decision, and the EU may not harmonise national citizenship law.[234] The European Parliament will enjoy the same right of consent where it is proposed to add to the list of EU

---

[233] Articles 18-25 TFEU.
[234] Article 19(2) TFEU.

citizenship rights, but national parliaments are asked to confirm the law.

In the case of an extension of the franchise for municipal and European Parliamentary elections, the Parliament will only be consulted about a Council law, where the Council acts unanimously. The same abnormal procedure applies to extending diplomatic and consular protection. However, a degree of flexibility is permitted if action should prove necessary to help citizens exercise their right to move and reside freely throughout the Union and the treaty has not provided the necessary powers. The ordinary legislative procedure is to be the way of plugging these gaps – without the Council unanimity required by the general 'flexibility clause' unless the measures directly affect passports, identity cards or social security identification.

There are fewer abnormalities in relation to the new treaty's treatment of the organisation and management of the single market, including the free movement of persons and services, freedom of establishment, freedom to provide services, the free movement of goods, the customs union, prohibition of quantitative restrictions to trade, free movement of capital and payments, competition policy, state aids policy, taxation policy and approximation of laws. The Council retains its executive power, on a proposal of the Commission, to adopt regulations and decisions in social and economic policy.[235] On the same basis the Council fixes tariffs and duties, and may take emergency action to safeguard against instability caused by unusual flows of capital or to freeze the assets of terrorists. The Council adopts regulations, on a proposal of the Commission and after consulting the Parliament, on companies' abuse of dominant positions in the internal market, cartel operations and other anti-competitive behaviour, including state aids to industry. Where the Union has exclusive competence, the Commission has the executive power to run the competition and state aids policies.

---

[235] Article 26(3) TFEU.

As far as changes in legislative procedures are concerned, QMV replaces unanimity in the Council for laws concerning the freedom of movement for self-employed people and the mutual recognition of their professional qualifications.[236] The new treaty also provides for legislation to strengthen co-operation between national custom authorities.[237] The ordinary legislative procedure is introduced for free movement of capital including foreign direct investment, financial services and capital markets regulation.[238] Any step backwards from liberalisation of third country capital movements must be taken by a Council law, with Council acting unanimously after consulting Parliament.

With regard to social security for migrant workers, including self-employed and workers' families, the UK laid down one of its notorious 'red lines'. Effectively, any one state will be able to block the legislative procedure.[239] Another thorny issue in the treaty revision negotiations concerned the harmonisation of taxes. The Union has already found it necessary to move towards the approximation of rates and structures of certain indirect taxes, notably VAT and excise duties on alcohol, tobacco and petrol. Although the principle of competition between tax regimes is generally adhered to, the Commission has sought to improve the smooth operation of the single market by reducing the very wide disparities in tax rates and structures that hitherto existed between states. Despite of earnest attempts to soften the decision-making procedure in Council, the British won another of their 'red lines' and unanimity is preserved as the general rule for tax matters, both indirect and direct.[240]

A new clause has been introduced to provide legislation for the uniform authorisation and protection of intellectual property rights. But decisions on the use of languages for the

---

[236] Article 53 TFEU.
[237] Article 33 TFEU.
[238] Article 64 TFEU.
[239] Article 48 TFEU.
[240] Article 115 TFEU.

filing of patents remains subject to a unanimous Council law, with the Parliament merely consulted.[241]

The ordinary legislative procedure is to be used for EU laws establishing incentive measures designed to encourage co-operation between member states in the field of employment policy.[242] QMV and co-decision will also be used to set minimum requirements for workers' health and safety, conditions in the work place, the information and consultation of workers, the integration of persons excluded from the labour market, equality between women and men with regard to labour market opportunities and treatment at work, the combating of social exclusion, and the modernisation of social protection systems.[243]

By contrast, the Council acts unanimously after only consulting the Parliament in relation to social security and social protection of workers, the protection of workers where their employment contract is terminated, the representation and collective defence of the interests of workers and employers, including codetermination, and the conditions of employment for third-country nationals legally residing in Union territory. However, with the exception of laws concerning social security and the social protection of workers – more UK 'red lines' – the Council may decide, acting unanimously on a Commission proposal and after consulting Parliament, to switch the remaining three items to the ordinary legislative procedure. Unlike the general *passerelle* clause, this sector-specific *passerelle* is not subject to the consent of national parliaments. As in the existing treaty, EU legislation does not apply to pay, the right of association, the right to strike or the right to impose lock-outs. And as before, there is to be provision for binding agreements at the EU level between management and labour which could foreshorten the legislative processes – and provide the framework for the kind of agreement between employers and

---

[241] Article 118 TFEU.
[242] Article 149 TFEU.
[243] Article 153 TFEU.

trades unions that was missing in the recent Finnish and Swedish cases.[244]

The Lisbon treaty extends the normal legislative basis for the operation of the European Social Fund.[245] Provisions on economic, social and territorial cohesion lay down the legislative basis for the European Regional Development Fund and the Cohesion Fund. The former provides targeted development assistance to all the poorer regions of the Union. The latter is designed to contribute to environmental projects and trans-European infrastructure networks in the poorer states. The extension of the ordinary legislative procedure to the setting of the tasks, priority objectives and organisation of what are known as the Structural Funds (Social Fund, Regional Development Fund, Agricultural Guidance and Guarantee Fund) as well as the Cohesion Fund is a big advance for the European Parliament. (The Treaty of Nice merely provides for unanimity in Council and Parliament's assent.)[246]

The other common policies

We have already noted the victory for Parliament in relation to the common agricultural policy and common fisheries policy. In both cases, although QMV has long been used in Council, Parliament has had hitherto only a consultative role.[247] The reform treaty gives MEPs equal power with ministers to shape the future direction and pace of CAP reform. Coupled with the abolition of the arcane distinction between compulsory and non-compulsory expenditure within the EU's annual budget, Lisbon rectifies what has been an unfortunate gap in the powers of Parliament to control what is, after all, the Union's most substantial and venerable common policy. There is no change to the Council's executive power to set, on a proposal of the Commission, the fixing of farm prices, levies, aid and quotas.

---

[244] Article 155 TFEU.
[245] Articles 162-164 TFEU.
[246] Article 177 TFEU.
[247] Article 43 TFEU.

EU policy on the environment is aimed at preserving, protecting and improving the quality of the environment, protecting human health, prudent and rational utilisation of natural resources, and promoting measures at international level to deal with regional or worldwide environmental problems. The ordinary legislative procedure pertains for environment policy with the exception of some anomalous items, where Council unanimity plus consultation continues to apply.[248] Again, however, the new treaty includes a sector-specific *passerelle* clause to allow the Council of Ministers, acting unanimously on a proposal of the Commission and after consulting the Parliament, to switch these items too to the ordinary legislative procedure, without a referral back to national parliaments.

No change is made to the Convention's provisions on consumer protection, which themselves closely followed the existing treaty.[249] The ordinary legislative procedure also applies throughout to the common transport policy and to trans-European networks. Parliament is to be consulted by Council in making regulations to outlaw discriminatory charging policies by carriers.[250]

The status of EU common policy for research and technological development gets a boost in the new treaty by the creation of a 'European research area'.[251] The ordinary legislative procedure is extended under the treaty to the design of the multi-annual research and development framework programmes, and the laying down of rules for the participation of researchers and the dissemination of results. EU legislation is also foreseen for supplementary programmes involving only a certain number of states. Parliament will be consulted in the making of Council regulations and decisions concerning the administration of the research programmes and in the making of Council laws

---

[248] Article 192 TFEU.
[249] Article 169 TFEU.
[250] Article 95 TFEU.
[251] Article 179(1) TFEU.

establishing the specific programmes. In a broadening of the common policy, space research wins explicit recognition.[252]

The last common policy in the field of shared competences concerns energy, where the common policy is intended to ensure the functioning of the energy market, the security of energy supply in the Union, the promotion of energy saving and efficiency, and the development of renewable forms of energy.[253] The treaty retains unanimity only for measures of a fiscal nature – that is, ecological taxation and excise duties on petroleum, diesel and aviation kerosene. Nevertheless, EU law will not affect a state's right to choose its own type of energy sources or the general structure of its energy supply. The Lisbon treaty does not touch materially the objectives or procedures of the Euratom Treaty of 1957 which regulates at the supranational level the use of nuclear fuel for civilian purposes. Five states made a declaration of their preference for another IGC to amend Euratom.[254]

In the area of supplementary competences, EU legislation precludes any harmonisation of national laws. The open method of co-ordination is preferred. The addition of public health to this category remains the most controversial because of the way fiscal policy impinges on the consumption of tobacco and alcohol. But the new treaty establishes firm legal bases for EU action against bio-terrorism, tobacco advertisements and health food. EU legislation will also be permissible to set high standards for the trade in medicine, human organs and blood, for measures in the veterinary and phytosanitary fields, and measures concerning the monitoring of cross-border threats to health. Laws will also be used to establish incentive measures to combat major cross border health scourges.[255]

---

[252] Article 189 TFEU.
[253] Article 194 TFEU.
[254] Declaration 54 by Germany, Ireland, Hungary, Austria and Sweden.
[255] Article 168 TFEU.

Similar provision for the open method of co-ordination is applied to the other policy sectors in this category, including industry, where the Union's policy objectives are to raise competitiveness by speeding up structural reform and to exploit research and innovation.[256] The ordinary legislative procedure replaces unanimity in the Council with respect to cultural policy, where the main goal of EU action is to improve knowledge of European history, to conserve Europe's cultural heritage and to foster artistic and literary creation.[257] The objectives of the new EU policy on tourism are to encourage good practice among states.[258] In the field of education, youth, sport and vocational training policy, the main thrust is to encourage youthful participation in the democratic life of the Union.[259] The priorities remain the development of the European dimension in education, particularly through language teaching, and the encouragement of teacher and student mobility. Sport gets a higher profile. In the field of vocational training, the priority is to facilitate the adaptation of the workforce to industrial change.

A new article provides for civil protection in the wake of natural or man-made disasters within the Union as well as 'promoting consistency' in international civil protection.[260] The clause provides the legal base necessary for the operations of the civilian arm of the European security and defence.

Finally, a new legal base is provided for administrative co-operation to ensure the more effective implementation of EU law, including the supervision of the financial sector and tax collection. The Union may support the exchange and training of national civil servants. Rather coyly, it adds that no state is obliged to avail itself of such support.[261]

---

[256] Article 173 TFEU.
[257] Article 167(5) TFEU.
[258] Article 195 TFEU.
[259] Articles 165-166 TFEU.
[260] Article 196 TFEU.
[261] Article 197 TFEU.

CHAPTER TEN   WILL THE UNION
              SOLVE THE CRISIS?

However well intentioned and skilful the drafters of the Treaty of Lisbon, practitioners quite reasonably want to know how the new constitutional arrangements will work in practice. What will be the impact of Lisbon on the day to day management of the Union? How will the reforms affect the shaping of public policy in Europe? And, in particular, will the new set up help the Union weather the current financial and economic crisis?

The social dimension

The drafters of the Lisbon treaty took steps to strengthen the social dimension of the single market. An important clause is included which deals with the treatment at the EU level of services of general economic interest, such as the gas, water and electricity industries.[262] The matter was hotly pursued by the European Trades Union Confederation (ETUC), representing most of Europe's powerful public sector trade unions. EU policies to boost competition within the single market, to facilitate cross-border trade and to limit state aids to industry, have long since ended the protection once accorded to nationalised monopolies. Provision is made for European legislation that will establish principles of universal access to general services and set conditions for their survival in the newly liberalised market place.

A new protocol on services of general interest was installed in the treaty, with a dual purpose. The protocol's first aim is to affirm the essential role and wide discretion of national, regional and local authorities in providing services of general economic interest in their highly diverse ways and according to their own standards of quality, affordability,

---

[262] Article 14 TFEU.

universal access and consumer rights. The second aim is to underline that the EU has no competence in the field of non-economic services of general interest, such as public health services. In perfect counterpoint, an adjoining protocol confirms that the EU has the power to take action to ensure that competition is not distorted within the single market.[263]

The elevation to mandatory status of the Charter of Fundamental Rights should not be over-looked, as it often has been, in the debate about the social dimension of the single market. Various trenchant articles of the Charter spell out workers' rights to information and consultation within their firm, the right of collective bargaining and strike action, the right to employment services, the right to protection in the case of unfair dismissal, the right to fair and just working conditions, the prohibition of child labour, the right to maternity and paternity leave, the entitlement to social security, unemployment benefit and social housing, the right to health care, access to services of general economic interest, and the right to environmental and consumer protection.[264]

Despite the inhibitions of certain states, including the UK, EU social policy legislation has been for many years a progressive influence. The image of the EU as a neo-liberal capitalist conspiracy against the workers is and always has been garbage. Nevertheless, the enlargements of the Union in 2004 to the eight countries from Central Europe and in 2007 to the two countries of the Eastern Balkans have given rise to new fears within the older member states about social dumping – that is, the displacement of higher paid local workers by lower paid immigrant workers. Large movements of migrant labour have taken place since 2004, especially of Poles moving to the UK and Ireland. The onset of recession in 2008 has reversed the flow as job opportunities dry up in the West. But the social impact of that sudden immigration of millions of fairly well qualified and eager to work, young EU citizens has had a lasting effect on public attitudes to enlargement. Today, regular Eurobarometer polls show a

---

[263] Protocols Nos 26 and 27, respectively.
[264] Charter Articles 27-38.

consistent and widespread view that the pace of the EU's recent enlargement is thought to have been too fast. (That view is not exclusive to the Western states: it also shapes Polish public opinion towards the possibility of Ukrainian membership.)

Several disputes against alleged social dumping found their way to the European Court of Justice. Two cases in particular dealt with the employment of workers from the Baltic states by Finnish and Swedish employers.[265] In December 2007, the Court found that, where national law does not otherwise provide, EU law cannot impose on firms collective labour agreements that go beyond the minimal requirements laid down in the posting of workers directive of 1996.[266] In 2008, after many years of difficult negotiation, the temporary agency workers directive was passed into law.[267] Fraught negotiations on the equally complex revision of the working time directive still continue.[268]

The impact of the economic recession in early 2009 was seen starkly in the placards of striking workers demanding 'British Jobs for British Workers'. Immigrants, or in this case, migrant workers from other EU countries, are the first to feel the political backlash when unemployment looms. Equally, the delocalisation of companies provokes nationalist ire. President Sarkozy stoked the protectionist flames when he sought to repatriate a Peugeot Citroen plant from the Czech Republic. 'If you build a Renault plant in India to sell Renaults to Indians, that's justified', he said. 'But if you build

---

[265] Case-438/05, ITWF & Finnish Seaman's Union v. Viking, and Case C-341/05, Laval v Swedish Building Workers' Union, December 2007.

[266] Directive 96/71/EC of 16-12-1996 concerning the posting of workers in the framework of the provision of services, OJ L 18, 21-01-1997.

[267] Directive 2008/104/EC of 19-11-2008 on temporary agency work, OJ L 327, 5-12-2008.

[268] Cercas Report (2nd reading position of European Parliament), 17-12-2008, P6_TA(2008)0615.

a factory ... in the Czech Republic to sell cars in France, that's not justified'.

For the European Union such extraordinary attacks pose a fundamental problem because the free movement of workers and of the establishment of a company are two of its core principles. While the mobility of firms and labour within the single market provides a necessary and welcome stimulus for Europe's economy, its social and political consequences command close attention. It was left to Czech prime minister Topolanek to remark bitterly about Mr Sarkozy: 'If someone wanted to really jeopardise the ratification of the Lisbon treaty, he could not have chosen a better way and a better time'.[269]

Economic governance

Alongside the debate over the social dimension of the internal market, lies the separate but connected question of economic governance, especially of the eurozone. Amid the financial turmoil, in January 2009, Slovakia joined the single currency as the sixteenth state to enjoy the full benefits of the world's largest market. Since its creation in 1999, when it incorporated eleven currencies, consumers and businesses alike have benefitted from the euro's stability-oriented policy framework, enhanced competition, cheaper borrowing and lower transaction costs. The euro has proved to be a remarkable stabiliser during the current financial crisis; it has emerged as a strong global currency. By combining a sound macroeconomic policy framework with an independent central bank, EMU has brought multiple economic benefits for its members: historically low inflation and interest rates, a boost to trade and investment, and, so the Commission claims, sixteen million new jobs.[270] The euro has also anchored stability in the euro area. As far as its members are concerned, it has eliminated the possibility of exchange rate

---

[269] Mr Sarkozy spoke on 5 February 2009; Mr Topolanek's reaction was published on 9 February (Agence France Presse and Hospodarske Noviny).
[270] Speech by Commissioner Almunia, Bratislava, 8 January 2009.

turbulence and speculative currency attacks. But that is not the whole truth about the euro.

European economic and monetary union was founded on the assumption that the single monetary policy was to be complemented by decentralised but co-ordinated national economic policies. Strict convergence conditions were set for joining the single currency in the first place, but the imperative to sustain the monetary union thereafter has relied largely on the presumption of financial and budgetary self-discipline and collective political will. The common interest rate is set at the federal level by the autonomous European Central Bank, whose central mission is price stability. National budgetary policy for eurogroup members has to conform to fairly strict guidelines, spelled out in the Stability and Growth Pact. But the states which adopt the euro continue with their own domestic tax and spend policies. In a crisis, there is to be no EU bail out of national defaulters. There is no provision for the centralisation of taxation beyond the fairly minimal programme to harmonise indirect taxes sufficiently (mainly VAT) in order to ensure the smooth operation of the single market, and to coordinate the fight against fraudulent tax evasion.

Unfortunately, once the euro had been launched successfully in 1999, many of the eurozone states failed to live up to their obligations to ensure fiscal discipline or to restructure their national economies to improve their competitivity. Cheap credit, lax banking regulation, inflated property markets and, from time to time, loose reporting of statistics combined to endanger the euro's early promise. Growing concern about the EU's laggard economic performance drove successive meetings of the European Council to establish a set of objectives – notionally to be achieved by 2010 – with the overall aim of boosting competitivity, productivity and employment. This came to be known as the 'Lisbon agenda', named after the European Council under the Portuguese presidency in March 2000. Its mission was to turn Europe into the 'most competitive and dynamic knowledge-based economy in the world capable of sustainable economic growth with more and better jobs and greater social cohesion'. It adopted an essentially liberal approach in which the 'open method of co-ordination', involving bench-marking, peer review, codes of conduct and the sharing of best practice between governments took precedence over economic regulation driven by the Commission.

Yet the ambitious goals of the Lisbon economic agenda have not been realised. The lack of management tools at the EU level to increase Europe's industrial productivity was compounded by the fact that the EU's own budget remained – and still remains today – relatively small. Efforts to liberalise labour markets and to defuse the 'pensions time bomb' caused by Europe's fast ageing population were spasmodic and, not least in Germany, highly controversial.

So far, the euro has survived the financial crisis so far with its reputation enhanced. Think of the vulnerability of the residual currencies – the punt, the lira, the peseta or the drachma – if the euro had not existed, and the case for a common currency is simply made. Yet the economic recession exposes the weaknesses as well as the strengths of the euro. The lack of coordinated economic policy to complement the single monetary policy, coupled with weak regulation, produces less than optimum results as far as the recovery is concerned.

The new European Commission, backed by a majority in the Parliament, can be expected to strengthen the grip on the conduct of the EU's broad economic policy. Under the Lisbon treaty, the ordinary legislative procedure is introduced for setting the detailed rules of the multilateral surveillance procedure.[271] The Commission wins the right to address a warning about a deteriorating fiscal situation directly to the state concerned.[272] It will also be able to make a formal proposal – in place of a mere recommendation – to the Council, which must act on it without delay, about whether

---

[271] Article 121(6) TFEU.
[272] Articles 121(4) TFEU on surveillance of broad economic policy guidelines and 126(5) on excessive deficits.

or not an excessive deficit exists.[273] However, the Commission has been frustrated in extending its powers to propose the actual measures which should be taken by a state in order to extricate it from a situation of excessive deficit. Supported by Britain from the sidelines, France and Germany, stung by criticism from Brussels for their lax budgetary policies, have been so far unwilling to accept an enhanced role for the Commission in the governance of the economic and monetary union. That is a pity.

In November 2008, the Commission established a group of experts under the leadership of Jacques de Larosière to examine and make proposals for a strengthening of the supervision of the EU's financial sector. Innovation is needed here. Greater supervisory powers for the ECB would exclude, importantly, the City of London, and in any case would lack transparency. Moreover, the Lamfalussy 'level 3' committees, set up to advise the Commission about the finance industry and made up of national regulators, do not encompass the whole spectrum of banking, securities market and insurance. Something new and better is needed to re-establish trust and improve transparency. At least the Lisbon treaty provides the flexibility that is needed for the Council and Parliament to enact regulations in this critical area.

The new treaty also boosts to some extent the autonomy of the eurogroup. This is a welcome reinforcement at a time when the expansion of the eurozone is being mooted even to some countries, notably Iceland, which is not even a member of the EU. The treaty lays down that a Council decision to allow a new currency to join the euro must be preceded by a positive recommendation from a qualified majority of current eurogroup members.[274] This effectively gives the eurogroup states full powers of co-option. The treaty lengthens the list of provisions that do not apply to states outside the eurogroup.[275] Eurozone members are intended to have a unified policy and will represent

---

[273] Article 126(6) TFEU.

[274] Article 140(2) TFEU.

[275] Article 139(2) (i) and (j), and Article 139(4) (a) and (b) TFEU.

themselves as one within the international monetary system.[276] They have decided to develop, significantly, ever-closer coordination of economic policies within the euro area, and, to that purpose, have formalised their previously informal ministerial meetings.[277] It was striking that the special meeting of eurozone leaders in October 2008, organised by Nicolas Sarkozy, was the first ever of its type. Once the new treaty comes into force, one should expect euro summits to become a regular feature of the EU calendar.

The latter development raises the important question of who precisely is the spokesman for the eurogroup on the international stage. There are three contenders for that role: the President of the European Central Bank, the Commissioner responsible for economic and monetary affairs, and the president of the eurogroup Council, Jean-Claude Juncker, who as Luxembourg's finance minister (as well as prime minister) has been elected twice for two and a half years to chair it and has been named, somewhat glibly, 'Mr Euro'. But this is a delicate matter, and requires each of the three to respect scrupulously the constitutional role of the others. Anything less could damage international market confidence in the euro. Mr Juncker has been characteristically scathing about the present incoherence, especially after President Sarkozy wilfully excluded him (but included Mr Barroso) from a crisis meeting of the G7 leaders in October 2008. 'The Chinese, the Americans, the others, I can assure you, ... find us ridiculous,' he said, adding that it was fortunate that 'being ridiculous doesn't kill you, otherwise the streets of Brussels would be covered in dead bodies'.

In July 2004, the Court of Justice clarified, at the request of the Commission, the respective roles of the Commission and Ecofin in the operation of the Pact. The Commission proposed that the Pact should be interpreted more flexibly and that the sanctions possible under the original version should be quietly dropped. It suggested that more attention

[276] Article 138 TFEU.
[277] Protocol No. 14 on the Eurogroup.

should be paid to debt sustainability in the surveillance of budgetary positions, as well as to the particular domestic circumstances of each state, in particular following periods of weak economic growth. The revised Stability and Growth Pact, underlining the importance of contra-cyclical policies, came into force in March 2005.[278]

The treaty revision had to deal sensitively with the Stability and Growth Pact, which continued to lose credibility as a result of its regular infringement. At Dutch insistence, a new declaration was inserted which confirms the Union's commitment to the Stability and Growth Pact.[279] The states promise to use periods of economic growth to consolidate public finances and improve their budgetary positions. Tentatively they admit that 'improved economic policy co-ordination could support this objective'. This is fairly feeble stuff.

The sterling crisis

The acute financial and economic crisis which was presaged by the decline of Northern Rock in the summer of 2007 and the fall of Lehman Brothers in September 2008 has triggered, among other things, a fall in the value of the pound sterling against the euro of over 20 per cent. This has rightly provoked a new debate about sterling's eventual membership of the single currency. At present, and since 1997, there has been something of a stand-off between sterling and the euro. Gordon Brown, as Chancellor of the Exchequer, invented five home-grown tests designed to prevent Tony Blair, as prime minister, from taking Britain in. Those tests, whose answers were expected to be unambiguous, concerned

---

[278] The Stability and Growth Pact consists of two regulations: Council Regulation 1055/05 on the strengthening of the surveillance of budgetary positions and the surveillance and coordination of economic policies – the preventive arm of the Pact, and Council Regulation 1056/05 on speeding up and clarifying the implementation of the excessive deficit procedure – the dissuasive arm of the Pact (OJ L 174, 07-07-2005).
[279] Declaration 30 on Article 126 TFEU.

sustainable convergence of the economies of the UK and the eurozone, the flexibility of eurogroup policy, investment, the City of London and employment.

A change of policy by the Labour government about the euro would change fundamentally the terms of Britain's engagement with the European Union. Although nobody could be certain about the timing of Britain's euro entry, still less about the level at which the exchange rate will stabilise for the requisite two year preparatory period, one would expect a firm declaration of intent to join by the British government to contribute directly towards that necessary stabilisation process, and to encourage the European Central Bank to address in its monetary policy the specific characteristics of the imbalanced and debt-ridden British economy.

There should be no doubt that a change of heart by the UK about sterling's membership of the euro would be popular with its fellow EU members. The dramatic fall of the pound has triggered cries of unfair competition from Britain's major trading partners. The Republic of Ireland is particularly exposed: one third of its exports go to the UK, and its Ulster land border is proving to be an irresistible temptation for Irish shoppers taking advantage of cheap sterling prices. The Irish finance minister Brian Lenihan has already remarked that it is more patriotic to pay taxes back home than to the Queen. If the sterling crisis continues indefinitely, and there comes no official reaction from the UK government, one can confidently expect fears to rise about the solidity of the single market.

As Britain reflects on what to do about sterling, so the rest of the Union is trying to draw the right conclusions about the euro. The ECB, under the cool guidance of Jean-Claude Trichet, has played a fairly steady hand since the crisis broke. The Bank's interest rate has been reduced from 4.25 per cent in October 2008 to 1.5 per cent at the time of writing. In this performance, the Bank is closely watched and quizzed by the European Parliament: over the decade there have been more than fifty appearances of the President of the ECB in front of MEPs. The EU's Parliament is right to insist on regular democratic checks over the ECB, while maintaining respect for its independence.

Economic recovery?

The EU must indeed be both agile and accountable if the economic crisis is to be turned into an opportunity. Coordination is the key to avoiding a deep and long lasting recession. At the European Council in December 2008, the states agreed to employ a coordinated budgetary stimulus amounting to 1.5 per cent of GDP. Of this figure, 1.2 per cent is to be financed at the national level. Crucial to the success of this economic recovery plan is its timing, its focus on stimulating demand. It is also designed to be temporary in order to avoid the need for permanent tax hikes. In the end, public finances have to be sustainable. Europe will have to return someday, and as soon as possible, to the disciplines of the Stability and Growth Pact. State bail-outs not only mean higher taxes for citizens but they also increase the temptation for banks to behave non-prudentially.

The Commission's new economic plan is certainly relevant to economic recovery, as are the new credit and investment facilities on offer from the European Investment Bank. But many of the smaller economies of central Europe – to say nothing of Iceland and Ireland – need more help. It is clear in these critical circumstances that size matters more than ever. The concept of the EU as a safe haven in time of trouble has never been more relevant. The EU has given loans of € 6.5 billion to Hungary in November 2008 and € 3.1 billion to Latvia in January 2009 as part of a package of measures coordinated with the IMF involving fiscal coordination and structural reforms to enhance competitiveness.[280] This kind of medium-term financial assistance is useful, but is as nothing compared to what will be needed if a member state of the eurozone were to default. Bailing out a defaulter is against the Maastricht treaty, but it

---

[280] These loans are agreed under Council Regulation 332/2002. The global ceiling for this facility has been raised to € 25 bn.

may become necessary to save the monetary union. If and when that happens, it will certainly be necessary to revise the treaty rules of the monetary union.

In addition to the stricter concertation of national fiscal policies, the European Union badly needs a new, and probably larger, budgetary policy. Only one fifth of the cost of the EU's recent recovery plan falls on the EU budget. It is still national treasuries – largely uncoordinated, sometimes incoherent and always jealous of each other – which predominate. The time for the floatation of an EU bond has arrived, and one hopes that such an idea will find its way into the reform of the EU budget which will get underway once the Lisbon treaty is in force and a new Commission has been appointed. As Mr Trichet says, the Stability and Growth Pact is a *quid pro quo* for not having a federal budget or a federal government.[281]

The current financial crisis has highlighted many weaknesses in the EU's supervisory framework, which remains fragmented along national lines despite the substantial progress achieved in financial market integration and the increased importance of cross border entities. If financial integration is to be efficient in terms of safeguarding systemic stability as well as in delivering lower costs and increased competition, it is essential to accelerate the reform of supervision. Supervisory reform has so far relied on an evolutionary approach, whereby the level 3 committees in the Lamfalussy framework are expected to achieve significant transnational convergence in supervisory practices and procedures. While a certain progress in convergence has been achieved, such progress has not allowed the EU to either identify or deal with the causes of the financial crisis. The existing national organisations lack a Union-wide framework for delivering convergence. The scope for effective macro-prudential oversight is limited.

The work in train of the high level group of Mr De Larosière is crucial to ending the mismatch between the

---

[281] Interview with the Financial Times, 15 December 2008.

reality of pan-European financial markets operating globally, on the one hand, and continuing national regulation, on the other. The group should also propose ways to reinforce cooperation between European supervisors and their international counterparts. The EU has already taken legislative steps to protect bank depositors, regulate the activities of credit rating agencies and strengthen rules on capital requirements. The EU must now assert its federal authority to take forward the integration of Europe's financial market.

Muddling through

As the Commission wisely suggests, better supervision and a single monetary policy together cannot provide the full stimulus needed by the European economy. Macroeconomic policies also need to support demand. The Commission's economic recovery plan brings together a fiscal stimulus to boost demand in the short term and a programme of smart investments to strengthen growth prospects in the medium and longer run, but its scale is relatively small.

The EU also needs to persevere with the Lisbon agenda to build a truly competitive economy. Investment, public and private, in training and innovation, plus structural reforms in the labour market and reduction of administrative burdens, will increase productivity and growth potential. The recession is not the time to fall further behind with reform, but, rather, to intensify it so that Europe emerges stronger from the crisis and better equipped to compete globally.

International coordination is essential to building a new financial architecture and anchoring stability in the global financial system. The G20 summit in London in April 2009 is an important opportunity to take stock. It would be desirable for G20 to set the objective of agreeing to set up a global network of prudential supervision across the currency zones. The UN conference in Copenhagen in December – the follow-on from Kyoto – is another chance for the EU to show the way forward towards global governance and to promote policies which not only combat climate change but also contribute to the solution to the financial and economic crisis.

Exceptional circumstances besides, the leaders of the European Union tend to muddle through from crisis to crisis and from one treaty change to another. Bold decisions made with more than short-term vision are rare. As Mr Juncker once said in another of his sardonic remarks, everyone knows what they have to do: the problem is that nobody knows how to win an election after doing it.

Empty rhetoric has never been silent in Europe: it is always easier to will the ends than to provide the means – especially during a crisis of the magnitude we now experience. Yet the Treaty of Lisbon offers Europe a real chance to equip itself with practicable government, in good times and in bad, beyond the nation state. It provides the instruments, the procedures, the potential – and, without doubt, the words – to render the politics of muddling through redundant. Strategies can be devised under the new treaty; checks and balances assured; laws passed and policies implemented. It only remains to close the deal.

CHAPTER ELEVEN   THE IRISH QUESTION

As all the world knows, the people of Ireland voted on 12 June 2008 to reject the Treaty of Lisbon by a majority of 109,964. 53.4 per cent voted No on a turnout of 53.1 per cent. Nobody who took part in the Irish referendum campaign could have been surprised by the result. The pro-treaty campaign, led by the government, was late and lacklustre. Few politicians or business leaders were able to argue the case for Lisbon with conviction or credibility. On the anti-treaty side, a strange ragbag of Sinn Féin, ultra-Catholics, trade unionists, farmers, US-style neo-cons and traditional British eurosceptics united to spin all sorts of stories about the iniquities of Lisbon, few of which coincided with veracity. If there was control of spending in the campaign it was not apparent, and the strange *galère* of non-parliamentary opponents of the treaty was given equal time and space in the media to that of the forces of the pro-treaty parliamentary establishment. As in all referendums, the Irish people jumped at their chance to act opportunistically, without obvious consequences to themselves or, indeed, to the government of Ireland. The future of Europe, or the fact that Ireland has profited hugely from EU membership, barely featured in the campaign. It is difficult to avoid the conclusion that the Irish people enjoyed exercising power without taking sufficient responsibility.

Why the Irish voted No

The top three reasons cited to opinion pollsters for voting No were ignorance about the treaty (and annoyance at the government's inability to make it comprehensible), fears about loss of national identity, and protection of Ireland's neutrality. Ireland is certainly a conservative place where nationalist currents flow unusually strong. While content to shelter behind NATO in the Cold War, Irish 'neutrality' against Anglo-US imperialism is a sentiment widely shared and much admired. That the Treaty of Lisbon will greatly strengthen the European Union's efforts to reach a common foreign, security and defence policy certainly contributed to its rejection.

Former Taoiseach Garret Fitzgerald complains that the Irish are too courteous to mention their disgust at corruption in high places. After long-winded speculation about his personal finances, Bertie Ahern eventually resigned as Taoiseach on 6 May 2008, leaving his successor Brian Cowen little time to get established before the referendum vote. The on-going enquiry into Mr Ahern's affairs reminded people all too clearly of the humiliating disgrace of his former Fianna Fáil mentor Charlie Haughey.

The Irish, being hugely hospitable, are also too polite to speak openly about their suspicion of foreigners. But in 2004 Ireland suddenly turned from being a country of emigration into a country of immigration, mainly from Central European EU states. Ireland's immigration grew from under 50,000 a year in 1999 to over 150,000 in 2007. By 2008, one in ten workers in Ireland were foreigners. The stimulus to the economy was welcome, but the cultural shock on the streets of Dublin, Cork, Limerick and Galway was palpable.

These three factors – neutrality, corruption and immigration – appear to have played a large part in turning voters against the Lisbon Treaty.

So, apparently, did the fact that, under Lisbon, the size of the European Commission is to be reduced. Under a system of equal rotation, after 2014, each state will lose a Commissioner once in every fifteen years. This was feared to be particularly detrimental to the interests of Ireland and other small states. It was lamentable that the pro-treaty forces failed to explain that sticking with the current Nice treaty would force – and as things stand still will – a reduction in the size of the Commission as early as November 2009.

Whatever the reasons for the Irish No, the result is devastating for the European Union both internally and externally. It has stalled in a dramatic way the efforts of the

EU, going back several years, to settle its constitutional future. European parliamentary democracy has suffered a big setback. Plans to make the governance of the Union more efficient and transparent are postponed if not lost altogether. And the EU will not after all enjoy the greater role in international affairs that was prescribed by Lisbon. Global leadership in climate change will be hard to assert. Progress in building common policies in justice and home affairs, including asylum and immigration, will be negligible. Further enlargement of the membership of the EU beyond Croatia is now impossible.

The grave consequences of the Irish No raise the question about why Ireland, and only Ireland, decided to risk ratification of this complicated EU treaty by popular vote. Elsewhere, shocked by the adverse impact of the negative referendums in France and the Netherlands in 2005, Europe's politicians have returned to the relatively safe haven of their national parliaments. Even Denmark and (post Blair) the UK successfully avoided referendums on Lisbon. Quite why Ireland still stuck to a referendum is far from clear. A much cited case of 1987, brought by eurosceptic Raymond Crotty against the Single European Act, is not the whole answer. In that judgment the Irish Supreme Court found that transfers of sovereignty from Ireland to the European Union only had to be sanctioned by referendum if their transfer had the effect of altering 'the essential scope or objectives' of the EU. At that stage, the introduction of a common foreign policy was deemed to necessitate a referendum.

The Treaty of Lisbon, however, makes no such innovation, but seeks merely to build upon the Union's existing scope and objectives. At no stage in the protracted constitutional negotiations that culminated at Lisbon was it seriously proposed to confer major new competences on the EU. Instead, the new treaty serves to clarify and rationalise the Union's current scope and objectives, notably in the fields of security and defence policy and justice and home affairs. What matters is to strengthen the capacity of the Union to act with efficacy in a more challenging world. This means concentrating on improving legal and political procedures, streamlining instruments and boosting the democratic legitimacy of the institutions. Even the Charter of Fundamental Rights, which in any case builds on the existing corpus of European rights law, is mandatory only within the context of the explicit competences of the EU and the powers of its institutions.

So the choice of a referendum in Ireland is not a constitutional matter but a product of its peculiar political system. Ireland's parliament is elected by a rare form of proportional representation, the Single Transferable Vote, which pitches MPs and candidates as much against their own party colleagues as against those from opposition parties. Localism is dominant, populism rife and pork-barrel politics customary. Party political forces are aligned more on the outcome of the Irish civil war in the 1920s than they are on contemporary ideology. And it is these political parties – Fianna Fáil and Fine Gael – which, having shuffled off the responsibility for taking the decision on Lisbon from parliament to people, were laggardly in beginning their official campaigns to persuade folk to vote Yes.

When, at last, the campaign got going, there seemed to be no single agreed over-arching message to unite the pro-Lisbon forces. Democracy and efficiency, as proffered by Lisbon, seemed rather abstract concepts. Some government ministers, as well as (alarmingly) the Irish European Commissioner Charles McCreevy proved to be badly briefed and scarcely motivated. The civil society organisation Alliance for Europe was small and weak. The social partners, farmers' organisations and churches were at best ambivalent in backing the case for Lisbon and at worst equivocating. And it remained unclear throughout the entirety of the campaign whether Lisbon was being sold by its supporters as a continuation of the status quo or as a radical improvement to what had gone before. One of the more telling posters of the No side, to which the government found no effective answer, proclaimed *'Keep Ireland strong in Europe: Vote No!'*. This strategic lapse by the Yes campaign was a cardinal error in a country which, rightly or wrongly, regards itself as being essentially 'pro-European' and which, by any standards, had done very well politically and economically as a result of its EU membership.

Membership of the EU has brought Ireland out of the shadow of the United Kingdom and has made many Irish rich. Ireland is a small country which has always managed to punch above its weight in EU politics. Nevertheless, while Ireland's EU membership may not be called into question, the pace and scope of future European integration is a sensitive issue in a country where nationalist and republican sentiment is still strong. Rural Ireland remains religious and conservative. Many feel the risk of Irish isolation on the western periphery of a Union that enlarges eastwards. Immigration has replaced emigration as the very public face of Europe – and just at the time that, economically, the Celtic tiger has lost her growl.

All these sensibilities were cleverly exploited by the numerous factions of the nay-sayers. It is of little comfort that most of the diverse and often contradictory arguments of the No campaign were pitched not at the reforms on offer under the Treaty of Lisbon but at the state of the current, unreformed EU. The powerful beef farmers, for example, opposed an agreement in the Doha Round talks that would lower the EU's import tariffs. Former trade Commissioner Peter Mandelson was criticised for allegedly pursuing his own, Anglo-Saxon, neo-liberal agenda at the expense of the cherished Common Agricultural Policy. Complaints at prohibitive anti-pollution measures being imposed from Brussels, involving pesticides and peat-cutting, were common.

Recent important case-law of the European Court of Justice, notably Viking-Laval, had alarmed trade unionists that their wages and jobs were at risk from cheaper immigrant labour, notwithstanding the fact that the circumstances germane to Latvians working in Sweden or Estonians in Finland did not apply in the Irish case. It was hardly mentioned that both the trade talks and the Court judgments were taking place under the present Treaty of Nice.

Other objections to Lisbon were completely groundless. Left-wingers claimed that Lisbon would impose nuclear energy on Ireland. Business people spread alarm about how the EU, under Lisbon, would force Ireland to raise its corporation tax. Nationalists insisted that Ireland's post-colonial 'neutrality' will be impossible to sustain under Lisbon. Right-wing Christians claimed that the Charter would authorise in Ireland abortion, euthanasia and gay marriage. A former pop star claimed that the Charter would reintroduce the death penalty. And a number of single issues with nothing whatsoever to do with Lisbon – for example, the threatened closure of a local hospital – inflated the anti vote.

The institutional questions were wildly distorted in the debate, particularly by people who should know better, like Sinn Féin and some independent MEPs. It was asserted, wholly without evidence that the treaty's hugely important democratic reforms would leave the citizen worse off than before. Irish eurosceptics also borrowed the lie of their British counterparts who claimed that Lisbon is somehow a 'self-amending' treaty. Quite what 'self-amendment' might be was never explained. The truth, as we have discussed above, is that there can be no future change to the EU treaties, however insignificant, without the unanimous agreement of all member state governments and also their national parliaments.

Battling against so much deception was always going to be difficult. For righteousness to triumph, it was essential for pro-treaty campaigners to nail two monstrous falsehoods. The first lie was that it was reasonable at one and the same time to be against the Lisbon treaty but to still support the European Union. The argument is, in other words, that the EU neither needs nor deserves this reform package. (Sinn Féin and the British Tories have more in common than meets the eye.) But the fact is that to reject Lisbon, as the Irish in their wisdom have done, means having to continue with the Treaty of Nice – which, paradoxically, eurosceptics universally hate. Without Lisbon the EU continues to exist, of course, but it continues to be weak in global affairs and clumsy in the domestic arena. With Nice, European parliamentary democracy remains only half-finished, the rule of law impaired and the system of government opaque. Putting more demands on an unreformed Union, for example in the field of climate and energy policy, or in the efforts to combat poverty and discrimination, will be futile. Without Lisbon, the EU is unable to deliver better public policy.

The second big falsehood of the 2008 referendum was that if Ireland were to say No, there would be something better on offer. This was never the case. Throughout the EU's protracted constitutional negotiations, very little consideration has been given – probably too little – to what would happen if ratification were to fail. Yet Irish No campaigners claimed that the 'period of reflection' established after the French and Dutch referendums had blocked the 2004 constitutional treaty had set a precedent for a further renegotiation of the Lisbon treaty text. This was dangerous self-delusion in a country which sports less than one per cent of the EU's total population. The fact is that, for the Union, France and the Netherlands are more important countries than Ireland. While it is impossible to think of the EU without France or Holland as founding member states, latecomers Ireland, Denmark and the UK are in a different league. When Denmark said No to Maastricht in 1992, ratification continued elsewhere, as it did a decade later with Nice when Ireland said No. So what had to be done in 2005 to get France and the Netherlands back on board was not going to be repeated for Ireland in 2008.

The 2004 constitutional treaty was already an amended version of the 2003 constitution drafted by the Convention of Valéry Giscard d'Estaing. The Lisbon treaty was a further modification of what is basically the same text. Both technically and politically it was always going to be impossible to contemplate yet another renegotiation simply because of the Irish. 'Plan B' is the Treaty of Lisbon – and the Treaty of

Lisbon is the best we can do. It is not perfect and, honestly, not pretty. Someday it too will need to be revised. But Lisbon is today's consensus. There is no agreement to do anything else – certainly not to embrace the neo-communist agenda of Sinn Féin or to surrender to the demagogic ravings of the ultra-nationalist right.[282]

In 2008, there really was no contingency plan about what to do if the Irish said No. Later, as we will describe below, the constitutional package was slightly re-wrapped for the sake of a second Irish referendum. But it is still the same Treaty of Lisbon inside. The refusal of Ireland's twenty-six partners to renegotiate the substance of Lisbon has been an impressive feature of political developments since the referendum, fully bearing out what was said during the referendum campaign itself. Surely Ireland will realise now that, in EU treaty terms, the only choice is between Lisbon and Nice.

The aftermath

In the immediate aftermath of the 12 June referendum, the European Union was in shock. How could a country which had done so well out of membership of the EU be so casual as to its future? At the June European Council meeting, Irish prime minister Brian Cowen earned no thanks for having no practicable proposals to make. The Irish problem seemed intractable. Assertions from EU governments elsewhere that the Irish No was an Irish problem and needed simply to be resolved in Ireland were hypocritical, irrelevant and anti-democratic. European interdependence is such that what we each do to our Union matters to everyone else. Ireland might have said No, but a large majority of member states were saying Yes. Ireland had wielded the legal veto, but did it have either the moral authority or the political clout to block constitutional progress for all the rest? The legal reality was one thing, and the Irish vote had been democratic. But it was asking the

---

[282] For Sinn Fein's view see www.no2lisbon.ie. For Libertas's view see www.libertas.eu.

impossible of Ireland's partners for them to respect the outcome. None could be complacent about the defeat of such an important treaty.

As the consequences of having to live with the Treaty of Nice sunk in over the summer, the mood darkened and irritation with the Irish grew. It became evident that, on examination, the so-called 'enhanced cooperation' procedures of Nice, which in theory allow a core group of states to go further and faster in any given area of integration, are in practice unworkable. Increasingly the realisation grew that Ireland now posed a very serious problem for the whole of the Union. Ireland's No had blocked European unification just at the time when European unity was needed more keenly than ever.

The European Union ended the summer in some anguish. On 30 July, the Doha Round collapsed. The stalling, if not the effective end of these complex multilateral trade negotiations was indeed, as Messrs Pascal Lamy and Peter Mandelson said, a collective failure by the global community. But the recriminations inside the EU, which is supposed to have a common commercial policy, have continued to poison the atmosphere in Brussels and, more pointedly, to mar the Union's attempt to shift spending away from agricultural support towards industrial productivity.

In August, the outbreak of war between Georgia and Russia further added to the Union's woes. Thanks largely to the activism of President Sarkozy, however, the EU quickly became the credible player in the efforts to broker a ceasefire and then to cope with Russia's new-found assertiveness. Efforts to develop an EU security and defence policy took on a fresh relevance, even beyond the stated aspiration of France's programme as EU presidency to concentrate on *l'Europe de la défense*.

EU-NATO relations came centre stage. President Sarkozy's decision to reintegrate France's military with NATO, the end of the Bush presidency in the US, and NATO's 60th anniversary summit in April 2009 provide the best opportunity, and possibly the last, for NATO to review its fundamental mission and organisation. Review is not only necessary because NATO risks failure in Afghanistan, but also because of the emergence, for the first time, of the EU's complementary efforts to build a security and defence dimension of its own.

Whatever other conclusions are to be drawn from the Georgian war, NATO has had to come to terms with the fact that its automatic further expansion eastwards will not be taken for granted by European public opinion. The EU badly needs to distinguish itself from NATO by counselling a halt to both Georgian and Ukrainian pretensions to NATO membership. If NATO is worth saving, it is worth keeping strong: membership of Georgia and the Ukraine would not contribute to its strength, at least for the foreseeable future. Both countries would be better off engaging more directly and deeply with the EU as its own neighbourhood policy and security strategy are fine-tuned in 2009. But what kind of EU will its neighbours be engaging with? A Union weakened by perpetual struggle over its own constitution, or one strengthened by the early passage of its reform treaty?

The Georgian crisis also helped to put into sharper relief the refusal of Ireland to ratify the new treaty among the principal features of which is the foundation of a security and defence dimension to the European Union. Another prize of Lisbon is the extension of the Union's legal competence into the supply side of energy policy, which even by itself requires a more sophisticated EU approach to the problems of the Caucasus than we have seen hitherto.

Faced with Europe's dramatic security crisis, the Irish position looks increasingly preposterous. Lisbon gives the European Union the wherewithal to do good in world affairs. Does Ireland really want to play no part in that effort?

The salvage operation begins

Much to President Sarkozy's evident frustration, the Irish stalled for time. Months passed without much sign of constructive activity in Ireland – but with a great deal of bitter recrimination between the defeated pro-Lisbon forces.

Brian Cowen and his Fianna Fáil party had a particularly difficult autumn, to put it mildly, as the embers of the lost referendum were raked over and the financial storm broke over Ireland. At their lowest ebb, the government botched the budget and sank below Fine Gael in the opinion polls.

Ireland's beleaguered government put great play on mounting yet another survey of public opinion in an attempt to find out why the naysayers had won. In fact this poll, conducted by Millward Brown IMS, adds very little to what close observers of the referendum campaign, supplemented by a Eurobarometer poll in the immediate aftermath of the vote, already knew.[283] IMS began their survey on 24 July, by which time one must assume that a certain sobering up had already taken place. 42 per cent excused themselves for having voted No on the basis of their lack of insight. Whereas 22 per cent of those who claimed to have been among the 862,415 No voters declared that Ireland's position had been strengthened as a result, a significant 20 per cent of those conceded that the result had weakened Ireland. Much of Europe's future now rests on the political evolution of that chastened 20 per cent of Irish No voters.

A considerable factor determining the disastrous outcome of the referendum was the constant bickering during the campaign among the five pro-European political parties. Since 12 June that bickering descended into open warfare, with spokesmen from the opposition Fine Gael and Labour parties calling on the government to demand substantive changes to the treaty before a second referendum were to be held. Another government party, the Progressive Democrats, bickered itself into extinction. Only in October was an agreement reached to set up a new cross-party parliamentary committee to consider Ireland's treaty options in a more considered way. Recriminations also broke out within the government itself, putting more pressure on

---

[283] Flash Eurobarometer 245, Post referendum survey in Ireland, 18 June 2008. Millward Brown IMS, Post Lisbon Treaty Referendum Research Findings, September 2008. Eurobarometer (EB Standard 70), January 2009.

Taoiseach Brian Cowen to save his own skin first and that of the Lisbon treaty only second.

Mr Cowen and his finance minister, Brian Lenihan, missed a huge opportunity in September to make public their appeal to their EU counterparts for urgent help in shoring up Ireland's fragile banking system. On the presumption that such an appeal could have been met with a quick, coordinated and constructive response from Brussels and Frankfurt, the Irish people would have been given an impressive demonstration of the EU's mission and value. Instead the Dublin government opted for panicky unilateral measures, ignoring EU state aid constraints, by offering 100 per cent state guarantees for even the worthless lending of all Irish banks. Thus Ireland was seen to set a new precedent in the EU for beggar-thy-neighbour policies. In addition to sending the wrong signals back home, this performance hardly served to instil confidence elsewhere in the EU about the capacity of the Irish government to do the right thing by Europe.

At the European Council meeting in October, Mr Cowen did no more than ask for more time. President Sarkozy made it clear he wanted a collective decision at the next meeting in December about the fate of the Lisbon treaty. He was backed in that by all twenty-six members of the fragile coalition of states who had already ratified or who still intended to ratify. No head of government dared to breach their collective understanding that there would be no renegotiation of the Lisbon treaty.

Unofficially, however, there was discussion of the elements that could form part of the December package designed to get the Irish electorate to change its mind. The main elements in that package seemed fairly clear: interpretative declarations galore – but no protocols that would need ratification by other states; possible Irish withdrawal from the European Defence Agency; and, most difficult to swallow, an agreement to postpone the eventual reduction of the size of the Commission *sine die* (or at least until 2019).

As part of the salvage operation, a bold presidency of the Council or Commission could even begin to spell out the seriousness of the consequences for Ireland and for the rest of Europe if the Irish failed to change their mind. Certainly, the Irish are unlikely to change their mind unless they understand that there are indeed serious consequences for not doing so. But here lies danger. One possible scenario comprises a new form of semi-detached but still viable EU membership for Ireland. But such semi-detachment might be just the thing that would appeal to the Irish, who would then again vote No to the Treaty of Lisbon. If, on the other hand, an alternative scenario were to threaten a more complete detachment of Ireland from the EU, Ireland's voters would be likely to react very badly not only by refusing to leave the Union but also by rejecting Lisbon again – leaving not only themselves, but also everyone else, stuck with each other grumpily, under the discredited Treaty of Nice.

CHAPTER TWELVE   PROBLEMS ELSEWHERE

One notes that it is the option of sticking with the Treaty of Nice that is preferred by the British Conservative party. At its annual conference in September 2008, David Cameron, the leader, and William Hague, shadow foreign secretary, made their position crystal clear. They expect to get back into government at the next UK general election, probably to be held in spring 2010. If Lisbon is not in place by then – in other words, if Ireland has failed to change its mind – the Tories will hold a referendum in the UK which will, without doubt, bury the Treaty forever. If Lisbon is in force by then, the Tories will insist on a renegotiation of the UK's terms of EU membership.

There is a most unfortunate precedent for a British renegotiation. In 1976, the then Labour government sought to overthrow the original terms of membership which had been negotiated by a Conservative government and confirmed, just one year beforehand, in the UK's one and only referendum. Labour's renegotiation was ill-conceived and badly handled. Nationalistic sentiment was fired up by the tabloid press at home, and many enemies were made abroad. Thence, in 1979, came Mrs Thatcher – and the rest (more or less) is history.

Back to the future, and what in 2010 would be acceptable to a europhobic Tory Britain could also be irresistible for a eurosceptical Fianna Fáil Ireland. The puzzle for Mr Cowen and his party, therefore, is how to avoid being forced into a post-colonial, mid-Atlanticist pact with the British Tories.

Meanwhile, all was not well with the Lisbon treaty outside the British Isles. Poland's eccentric and nationalistic President Kaczynski refused to sign the ratification instrument until Ireland votes again despite the fact that the Polish parliament has successfully endorsed the treaty.

Germany's federal president is still constrained from completing the ratification process until the German federal constitutional court in Karlsruhe sees fit to judge first one then two applications from an assortment of nationalists against the treaty. And ratification by the Czech Republic stalled irritatingly.

The Czech problem matters particularly because its government took over the presidency of the European Union from the French for six months on 1 January 2009. One of the main jobs of the Czech presidency is to help Ireland implement the plan, agreed in outline by the European Council in December, to salvage the treaty. So instead of being part of the solution, the Czechs have become part of the problem. The Czech presidency started badly, and will continue to lack credibility and authority unless and until its government secures the ratification of Lisbon.

In good times, a weak EU presidency may not matter very much. But these are bad times, and the Union was highly fortunate to have had France's superman Nicolas Sarkozy in charge during the second half of 2008. The contrast with Mr Sarkozy's successor, Czech prime minister Mirek Topolanek, could not be greater. It is a contrast sharpened by the entirely coincidental arrival on the scene of America's own superman, Barack Obama, with an agenda of change. To many, Europe's leadership seems to be going in just the wrong direction at a time of acute global crisis.

It is not that middling sized countries such as the Czech Republic cannot run good EU presidencies: many have. And there is a good crop of energetic Czech ministers entirely capable in normal circumstances of managing the routine business of the EU Council and of properly being held to account in the European Parliament.

The issue is, rather, whether the Czech Republic has yet come to terms with its membership of the EU. As the first of nine ex-Warsaw Pact countries to take the helm of the Union, the question has rather wide ramifications. One leading Czech senator likened Mr Sarkozy's mini-summit, at the height of the financial meltdown in October, to a 'gathering of the four Powers of Munich' – that is, of Messrs Chamberlain, Daladier, Hitler and Mussolini in 1938. The author of this slander against the current crop of Europe's top leaders was a senior member of the governing Civic Democrats (ODS). The remark produced no reaction at all from other Czech senators, most of whom seemed to be labouring from deep illusions about the Lisbon treaty heard otherwise only on the wilder shores of rightwing europhobia.

One has come to expect the parliaments of former communist states to be assertive. Slender majorities and febrile political parties make governing difficult in Central Europe. The Czech senate raised a petition in the constitutional court against the Lisbon treaty, requesting a judgment on whether the EU treaty conforms with the constitutional character of the Czech Republic 'as a sovereign, unitary and democratic, law-abiding state'. The notoriously nationalistic Czech president, Vaclav Klaus, founder of the ODS, joined the case against the 'dead document' of the treaty and the 'useless document' of the Charter of Fundamental Rights (which Lisbon makes mandatory). In a somewhat erratic submission to the court, Mr Klaus inveighed against the creation of a European federal state, which, he asserted, will be advanced by Lisbon. He attacked some general principles of European integration, including that of European citizenship. For Mr Klaus and his fearful followers, it appears that democracy can only be national and sovereignty is not to be shared. They reject the concept of deepening interdependence between EU member states.

It was truly astonishing that the President of the Czech Republic should mount a veritable attack on continued Czech membership of an EU governed by the Treaty of Lisbon. Mr Topolanek's government made a full and fluent response to the constitutional court which was designed to convince any fair-minded judge that the Czech national interest is best served by strengthening rather than weakening the EU.

The court's judgment was postponed while President Klaus went on a (pre-planned) state visit to Ireland. In

Dublin Mr Klaus raised the stakes by dining very publicly with the anti-European demagogue Declan Ganley, who led the No campaign in the first Irish referendum, and other eurosceptics. Mr Ganley was fishing for Czech politicians to join an envisaged new group of rightwing nationalists in the European Parliament after June's elections.

Mirek Topolanek, meanwhile, had to work hard to keep hold of his leadership of the ODS and his premiership. He successfully survived a critical Congress of the party on 6 December, but conceded that the issue of the Lisbon treaty should be linked to a positive vote of parliament on the deployment of the US anti-missile radar system on Czech soil. That pledge sounded like an act of desperation at the time it was made, but it has become even more bizarre since as the new US administration of Barack Obama seems itself ambivalent about deploying the missile defence system. In the Czech parliament, where the radar issue divides government and opposition, a three-fifths majority is needed for the treaty ratification in both Houses.

The Czech court decides

The heads of government gathered again in Brussels on 11-12 December 2008 to deliberate on the fate of the Treaty of Lisbon. The context for their deliberation was inevitably affected by the deepening economic crisis, and the evident disagreement, not least between France and Germany, about what to do next by way of economic recovery. But the European leaders could not avoid, even if some had wanted to, the question of how to salvage the treaty.

Two recent developments had encouraged the summiteers to be bold. On 26 November the constitutional court of the Czech Republic dismissed the six objections to the treaty that had been raised by the Czech Senate, supported by the President of the Republic, Vaclav Klaus. The judgment, which was unanimous, cleared the way for the Czech parliament to proceed to ratify the treaty – but it has wider value too as the whole European Union tries to come to terms with its own constitutional ambitions. The court, led by the judge-rapporteur Vojen Güttler, determined as follows:

1. The treaty does not grant the EU a general competence to decide on its own competences (*'kompetenz-kompetenz'*). In other words, Lisbon will not turn the Union into a federal state. In fact, the new treaty creates a sufficiently certain normative framework for the pooling of Czech sovereignty within the EU for a number of defined purposes without risk to the constitutional core of the Czech Republic.

2. Member states remain masters of the EU's constitution because any treaty change has to be agreed by unanimity. A 'flexibility clause' -- which so affronts the nationalists -- grants to the Council of Ministers, acting by unanimity, the right only to adapt the powers of the institutions to new circumstances in pursuit of the objectives of the Union as set down in the treaty. The controversial article cannot be used to circumvent the limitations placed by the treaty on the competences of the Union.

3. The equally controversial *passerelle* or bridging clause merely allows for the European Council to decide, again by unanimity, to change a unanimous decision-making process into one governed by qualified majority. In the area of criminal law any member state retains a veto. And national parliaments become more involved in sanctioning the decisions of their respective governments.

4. The Union's capacity to conclude international agreements, although important, does not transgress Czech constitutional prerogatives as such agreements cannot stray to

cover issues outside the EU's conferred competences, either internal or external.

5. The standard of domestic protection of human rights is not adversely affected by making binding the EU's Charter of Fundamental Rights. The Charter does not expand the scope of EU law beyond the conferred competences. The accession of the EU to the European Convention on Human Rights (as provided for in the Lisbon treaty) will strengthen the supervision of human rights by and within the Union. The Charter, moreover, must be applied with full regard to the constitutional traditions of the member states.

6. The values and principles laid down in the Lisbon treaty and the Charter are wholly compatible with those enshrined in the Czech constitution. In so far as Czech state sovereignty is concerned, sovereignty is not an end in itself but is a means of fulfilling those values and principles.

The Czech constitutional court concluded that even with Lisbon the European Union will not be a federal state but will remain a unique type of organisation under international law. So there is no constitutional requirement to have recourse to a referendum in the Czech Republic, bypassing parliament.

Bearing the responsibilities of the presidency of the European Union, the Czech government should highlight to its parliament and people how the Treaty of Lisbon improves on the present Treaty of Nice. Taking a leaf out of the Irish debate, the government can promise always to ask parliament's future permission before agreeing in the European Council to the deployment of the treaty's flexibility clauses which allow for more qualified majority voting. Ministers must explain and defend the principle whereby the Union only enjoys competencies expressly conferred on it by treaty. Mr Topolanek should keep his ODS party firmly within the ranks of the mainstream centre right in the European Parliament.

Above all, the Czech government must shatter the widespread delusion that if Lisbon is sunk there will be something better around the corner. There won't. Lisbon is as good as it gets for Czechs as well as Irish. Mr Topolanek did not help matters during his first appearance as President of the Council at the European Parliament (13 January) when he told astonished MEPs that he found the Treaty of Lisbon worse than the Treaty of Nice. It was later explained that the prime minister was trying to make a joke. If Mr Topolanek improves his jokes he may yet rescue his term as EU president. If he does not, the four Powers of Munich may be back with a vengeance.[284]

---

[284] President Vaclav Klaus made no jokes at all when he spoke to the European Parliament on 19 February 2009.

CHAPTER THIRTEEN THE LAST CHANCE

The day following the judgment of the Czech court in Brno, the Irish parliament in Dublin published the result of its own enquiry into Ireland's EU predicament. The report of the special sub-committee of the two Houses of the Oireachtas was informed, measured and fairly conventional.[285] Would that Ireland's parliament had acted as decisively in advance of the June 2008 referendum rather than in its wake.

Chaired by Fine Gael Senator Paschal Donohoe, the enquiry had taken evidence from many of the shakers and movers in Europe's constitutional debate[286]. Submissions from those of non-Irish nationality provided a usefully broader spread of opinion than that which had been heard in the referendum campaign itself. To that extent, the Irish parliament succeeded in subtly changing the context of the subsequent debate – and, predictably, the report's decisively pro-Lisbon conclusions were decried even before its publication by Irish opponents of the treaty. (Sinn Féin and an independent but anti-Lisbon senator were members of the sub-committee, which did not fail to take evidence from anti-European elements, including Mr Declan Ganley.) What was just as significant about the exercise, however, was that it shifted the focus back to parliament and away from the extra parliamentary terrain. Furthermore, it provided the government with some significant cross-party insurance that had been largely lacking until that moment: Fine Gael and

---

[285] *Ireland's future in the European Union: Challenges, Issues and Options*, Houses of the Oireachtas, Sub-Committee on Ireland's Future in the European Union, Dublin, 27 November 2008.
[286] The Sub-Committee was much influenced by an authoritative report from the Institute of International and European Affairs, *Ireland's Future After Lisbon: Issues, Options, Implications*, Dublin, November 2008.

Labour spokesmen were complicit in, and evidently satisfied by, the work of the special sub-committee.

What did the enquiry conclude? First, it observed that, contrary to the claims of the anti-Lisbonites, Ireland's standing in the EU had diminished since the result of the June referendum. And what had been an immediate adverse reaction to the negative referendum was likely to get more, and not less, hostile as time passed. Irish business interests, in particular, feared a loss of foreign direct investment. The scenario of a two tier Europe, with Ireland marginalised on the periphery, 'would have a devastating effect on Ireland's political influence, economic prospects and international standing'.[287]

The report neatly exploded the most popular misapprehensions evidenced in the referendum. No, Lisbon would not affect Ireland's control over its own taxation policies. Yes, the EU was indeed committed to the protection of workers' rights as well as sustainable economic growth. Yes, Lisbon provides for member states to continue to deliver their own public services at the national and local level. No, the EU does not have competence over abortion, euthanasia or gay marriage. Yes, Irish neutrality will be maintained under Lisbon for as long as Ireland wishes to maintain it; and there is no provision for an EU army to conscript Ireland's sons and daughters.

On the matter of the Irish Commissioner, the report was clear-cut:

> 'While it seems that the purpose of the Commission is sometimes misunderstood, it does appear that having a Commissioner nominated by the Government is a matter of national sensitivity. While this Commissioner would not represent the Irish Government within the Commission, he or she can act as a conduit for the Commission in understanding any sensitivities which are particular

---

[287] Oireachtas report, p.3.

to Ireland. This serves both the Commission and Ireland. Having a Commissioner all the time would also offer legitimacy to the proposals made by the Commission.'[288]

On the vexed question of what to do next to restore Ireland's position in the mainstream of European integration, the sub-committee was less decisive. Having had a look at Denmark's numerous opt-outs from key areas of policy making – obtained as a result of the negative Danish referendum on the Treaty of Maastricht – the report concluded that 'opt outs are not cost free'. Indeed, the effect of opting out of the entire policy sector of security and defence (as proposed, for example, by Sinn Fein) would be to deprive Ireland of the use of its national veto. All in all, the report judged that to have to negotiate a looser form of Irish membership of the Union would be 'catastrophic' (for Ireland).

While the Oireachtas report delicately avoided any serious critique of the poor quality of the pro-Lisbon campaign earlier in the year, it did find that Ireland's public information and civic education policies are at fault in lacking a decent European dimension. It also levelled criticism at the government for failing to explain and justify EU legislation to the Oireachtas or the media. And it proposed various practical ways in which the Oireachtas itself could improve its scrutiny of EU affairs in order to counter a serious 'accountability deficit'. A 'scrutiny reserve' mechanism similar to that in use in the British parliament was recommended. Under this special procedure, British ministers may be obliged to delay casting the UK's vote in the Council of Ministers until they have reported back to the Westminster parliament.

The exercise by the Irish parliament in taking an unusually comprehensive view of the state of play of its country's relationship with the European Union is relevant to

---

[288] Oireachtas report, p.5.

a wide audience. Few other national parliaments have organised themselves to take such a similar strategic approach. The House of Commons, for example, voted to ratify the Treaty of Lisbon without the benefit of a thorough committee enquiry into its merits and demerits. (The British parliamentary debate was almost entirely restricted to the subsidiary question of whether or not there should be a referendum.) Other parliaments would be wise to take note of several aspects of the Irish report.

It was concluded, for example, that if Lisbon were not to be ratified, the intergovernmental character of the EU would grow to the detriment of the Community method. This was thought to be of special disadvantage to smaller member states, like Ireland and the Czech Republic. It was also noted that the jurisprudence of the European Court of Justice would tend to follow the broad policy direction defined by the core of the Union and not by the more marginal members.

> 'If Ireland does not play an active part in the framing of EU law, the law will develop without us and Ireland will not be in a position to shape it.'[289]

On the question of voting rights in the Council, the report argued that because, under Lisbon, a qualified majority will have to consist of at least 55 per cent of states (as well as 65 per cent of population) the interests of small countries against the big were adequately protected. In addition, the provision that a blocking minority can be formed of only four states was designed to reassure small states that the large will not have it all their own way.

> 'The Sub-Committee again notes that it is not voting power that gets results for Ireland, it is our influence.

---

[289] Oireachtas report, p.27.

It is not about votes but about being at the table with our good standing and influence intact.'[290]

The European Council acts

Brian Cowen arrived in Brussels on 11 December reinforced and encouraged by the work of the Irish parliament. To prepare for the summit he had been on a hectic bilateral tour of all the major capitals, and not least Paris. The agreement between the Irish Taoiseach and the French President was a surprise to those who had been led to expect the European Council merely to scope the options of a deal, invoking a bit of seasonal melodrama. This would have left the embattled Irish leader to declare his struggle victorious only in June or July 2009, once the municipal and European Parliamentary elections were out of the way. But the strong leadership of Nicolas Sarkozy propelled the deal to be done there and then. Or did it?

The ebullient performance by President Sarkozy in the European Parliament (16 December) rather glossed over the complexity of the question of how to salvage the Lisbon treaty. On the face of it, Mr Sarkozy had done well at the European Council the previous week. The Irish premier committed his government to having a second crack at ratifying the treaty. Something of a scandal occurred when Mr Sarkozy had suggested just such a thing during his trip to Dublin in July, in the immediate aftermath of the referendum. But what had scandalised in the summer was accepted quite calmly in the winter. The minutes of the European Council record that the Irish government 'is committed to seeking ratification of the Treaty of Lisbon by the end of the term of the current Commission' – that is, by 31 October 2009.[291]

The package deal agreed between the Taoiseach and his fellow heads of government consisted of four elements. First,

---

[290] Oireachtas report, p.44.
[291] Paragraph 4 of the Presidency Conclusions of the Brussels European Council, 11-12 December 2008.

contrary to the provisions of the both the treaties of Nice and Lisbon, the European Commission is to continue to have one member drawn from each of the EU's state nationalities. Such a radical departure from the decision to reduce the size of the Commission to eighteen is technically possible only under the terms of Lisbon and not of Nice. But this reversal of policy is a big concession by those more federalist EU states which have long argued that a smaller Commission will be more efficient and less likely to be dominated by vested national interests. It also marks a concession by the larger states which had already traded in a second Commissioner and accepted fewer seats in the European Parliament as their contribution to the Union's overall constitutional settlement. (The Chancellor of Germany, which is both federalist and large, was remarkably quiet during the discussion of this item.)

There are, of course, respectable arguments on both sides. Commission Vice-President Margot Wallström, in a departure from the official Commission line, has long believed that what a small Commission would gain in efficiency it would lose in legitimacy. It is certainly true that the formula of Lisbon, which would have introduced a system of equal rotation in the Commission among the states, would have left the college from time to time without a French citizen inside it. It is, in truth, quite difficult to conceive of a Commission that would work well without a Frenchman.

It is also true that Ireland's representatives in the constitutional talks have always complained about their possible exclusion from the Brussels executive. No doubt the Irish complaint has had something to do with having been deprived historically of an Irish minister of nationalist bent in the imperial government in London.

Yet it would be foolish to think that December's summit has resolved the issue of large versus small in the Commission for all time. A Commission of more than thirty members will not work unless a hierarchy is established internally of senior and junior Commissioners. It is not difficult to guess which states will seldom if ever be able to boast a senior member of the college. Furthermore, if the inflated Commission were ever suspected of operating in a manner detrimental to the interests of the large states, one can anticipate that the larger states would insist on the ascendancy of the European Council and the diminution of the role of the Commission into little more than that of a secretariat.

The second part of the Cowen-Sarkozy deal is that 'necessary legal guarantees' will be formulated with the aim of ensuring that Ireland will continue to be free to make its own decisions in matters of taxation, neutrality and family law. This concession to Ireland, at the instigation of its attorney-general, went farther than expected. Nobody knows quite what a 'necessary legal guarantees' are – but one presumes they must go farther than the anticipated (and perfectly acceptable) non-binding declarations that would simply interpret the treaty in the Irish context. The fact is that the treaty already means what it says, and gives ample safeguards to Ireland by way of opt-outs on defence policy, Schengen, justice and home affairs. The treaty confers on the EU only certain competences, which are clearly defined. The Charter of Fundamental Rights is binding only within the scope of those conferred competences and within the limitations of the institutions' treaty-based powers. Over-interpretation can lead to misinterpretation. One waits with interest to see how the legal experts will make a legal guarantee out of a truism.

Mr Sarkozy confidently told the European Parliament that a protocol or two can be glued on to the next EU treaty after Lisbon, which is expected to be the Croatian accession treaty. But the procedures for the EU's enlargement to Croatia are less ponderous than those for a constitutional revision of the type required by Ireland.[292] A hybrid treaty that attempted to deal with both Croatia and Ireland would risk being knocked down by the European Court of Justice. On the other hand, an Irish protocol bound as an

---

[292] Article 49 TEU for enlargement as opposed to Article 48 for constitutional change.

afterthought to the Lisbon treaty itself would trigger a new intergovernmental conference in the course of 2009 (risking a wider renegotiation) followed by national ratification, yet again, in all twenty-seven member states. The only practical option is that a pre-cooked protocol is added at some unspecified future date to the Treaty on European Union and the Treaty on the Functioning of the Union once Lisbon is safely in force. The opportunity to do this might still be several years ahead. In the meanwhile, Ireland will be asked to take it on trust that such a manoeuvre will eventually take place.

There is a precedent. In 1992, when the Danish referendum had blocked the entry into force of the Treaty of Maastricht, an elaborate package was concocted, involving a decision of the heads of government made under international law (rather than EU law), alongside two declarations of the European Council and a unilateral declaration by Denmark. These arrangements were codified in EU primary law only in 1997 when a fourth Danish protocol (it already had three) was added to the Treaty of Amsterdam. But the Danish precedent is not wholly apt because Denmark was seeking, and getting, real opt-outs – a course not open to Ireland today.

The Irish themselves have also got form. After their first referendum rejected the Treaty of Nice in 2001, a unilateral declaration by Ireland on defence issues was tied to a revision of the Irish constitution and successfully endorsed in a second referendum in 2002. The European Council duly took note of the Irish National Declaration.[293] Subsequently, the Lisbon treaty includes a protocol which reinforces the fact that it does not affect the Irish constitutional position on abortion.[294]

A further element of the deal at the European Council is that 'high importance' will henceforward be attached to social progress and the protection of workers' rights. This was a hard nut for Britain's Labour prime minister Gordon Brown,

---

[293] Declaration by the European Council, Seville, 21 June 2002.
[294] Protocol No. 35 on Article 40.3.3 on the Constitution of Ireland.

in particular, to swallow. Negotiations went on all night between officials before the British were reassured that this new posture of the European Council would not materially affect the standing of the EU in domestic labour law. At the same time, the Irish had to be given satisfactory confirmation that the treaty does not mean that the right to deliver public services of general interest will be surrendered to Brussels.

Lastly, as always at these events, seats in the European Parliament were traded to sweeten the deal. The Parliament elected in June 2009 will have 736 MEPs. Thereafter, once Lisbon comes into force, another eighteen MEPs will fill the extra seats foreseen in that treaty. In addition the three German MEPs of Nice who were to be sacrificed by Lisbon will enjoy a stay of execution for the remainder of the mandate. So the final total size of the Parliament 2009-14, excluding any Croats or Icelanders who might pitch up, will be 754. A tricky agreement will have to be reached about how to choose the extra eighteen MEPs and when exactly they should present themselves. Moreover, the principle of degressive proportionality which is supposed, under Lisbon, to guide the distribution of seats between states is once again abused. Parliament will have to insist that the derogation from primary law is only temporary, until 2014, by which time a radical overhaul of Parliament's electoral procedures will have to be agreed. Ideally, that reform is expected to introduce, in addition to the bulk of MEPs elected from national or regional lists, a small number elected from a single, transnational constituency.

Making the deal stick

Once back from their election, MEPs will be bound to take a hard look at the timetable and procedures for the appointment of the new Commission. Parliament will be unhappy to begin the election of a new Commission in July without knowing what the competences of the Union and the powers of the institutions are eventually to be. And, although it can be assumed that José Manuel Durao Barroso will be nominated for a second term as Commission president, it will only be once the Irish have voted again in October that the European Parliament will know about the final size of the college. The transitional arrangement eventually to be decided matters too to Mr Barroso: under Nice he needs to get the backing of a simple majority of the Parliament; under Lisbon he needs an absolute majority.

What was not discussed at the December European Council was how the Irish government and the other pro-Lisbon political parties could improve in 2009 on their campaigning performance in 2008. It should have been. The rest of us need to know what lessons have been drawn from the 2008 debacle. There is a legitimate interest across the EU in knowing if Ireland intends to reform its own laws about the conduct of referendums, not least with respect to the size and transparency of funding and the share-out of broadcasting airtime. Moreover, if each member of the European Council is to accept individual responsibility for their collective decisions, other heads of government might wish actively to help Mr Cowen in the campaign itself. Whatever the level of the participation of other EU governments, the European Commission and European Parliament in the Irish campaign, it would be important to get the line at once right and coherent. Differences of interpretation of this or that treaty clause in London, Paris or Berlin will provide valuable ammunition for the anti-Europeans in Ireland. It is indicative of the dilemma faced by Ireland's partners that in 2009 the Commission trebled its communications budget for Ireland, and has designed a special communications strategy to target Irish women, young people and low-income families.

The decision of the European Council to make the Irish vote again on the Lisbon treaty has been greeted with predictable squeals of outrage from Europe's nationalists of left and right. A broad majority of the Irish themselves, however, seem less fazed by the prospect of yet another exercise in the populist democracy. After all, Ireland had to vote twice on the Treaty of Nice. The second vote on Lisbon will be Ireland's seventh EU poll in twenty-two years. During that same period, there have been two Irish referendums on divorce (1986 and 1995) and three on abortion (1983, 1992 and 2002). The Irish are rather fond of a bet. Just as regular elections are the stuff of parliamentary democracy, referendums have to be frequent to fuel a plebiscitary democracy, as they are in Switzerland. Ireland is a hybrid between the Swiss system and that which prevails elsewhere in the EU. Unless and until Ireland chooses to regularise its method of ratifying EU treaty change in conformity with the constitutional practices of its partners, Europe's future direction will continue to be held hostage by the regular punt of the Irish electorate.

The need for logic

We have come a long way from the Congress of Europe in 1948. Yet the story of the still unfinished, troubled birth of the Treaty of Lisbon highlights the need for renewal in the European Union. In strictly institutional terms, of course, Lisbon brings the very renewal that is so urgently needed if Europe as a whole is to resolve its own problems of insecurity and division, let alone contribute more to meeting some of the challenges to Europe in the wider world. Lisbon brings Europe closer than ever to that elusive goal of unification which has tantalised European rulers of many types over the ages. This time the unity will be of a federal type, where power is shared between different levels of government and in which no level can exercise unfettered supremacy over the other.

The constituent parts of the European federation are the states that have been left standing at the end of the twentieth century, the bloodiest century in European history. Many of those states – Great Britain, France, Holland, Belgium, Spain, Portugal – have an imperial past abroad. Others – Austro-Hungary, Sweden – have an imperial past closer to home. Some are themselves federations of former principalities, smaller nations and regions. Most states emerged exhausted and impoverished from the wreckage of two world wars and the Nazi and Stalinist tyrannies. They found renewal in the creation of and accession to the European Community and its successor, the Union. Almost all states had fought each other for many hundreds of years, and some, like Ireland and Poland, had been subjugated. François Mitterrand once observed that France had been at war with all the other (then) fifteen member states of the EU except Denmark – and he could never quite discover why the Danes had never fought the French.

So the European Union is already a magnificent achievement, especially for older generations. But for the young, who voted No in large numbers against Lisbon in Ireland and against its predecessor treaty in France and Holland, the fact that the EU has made war out of date is not a sufficient incentive to identify with the Brussels institutions. Modern folk have other preoccupations which, indeed, are also highly relevant to whether the EU continues to be a success. But the connection has yet to be made between the authority of the EU and the anxieties and aspirations of many of its citizens.

This book has been mainly about treaty making. But it is obvious that post-national democracy cannot be built on treaties alone. Europe needs its citizens to become more actively involved in sustaining the effort at European integration. The EU is in no way doomed to succeed. Its unity may very well fracture if the ever-present forces of nationalism defeat those who are committed to making Europe more united along federal lines. Integration itself is a complex process, and has no obvious political finality. It works well in terms of business and finance: the single market and the single currency have helped Europe to become more stable and prosperous than ever before. Integration works quite well in terms of diplomacy and technocracy: the national and regional governments of the twenty-seven member states of the Union are functionally interdependent, and have learned to operate fairly well in finding common solutions to shared problems. In sport and culture, European identity is already quite strong, and many Europeans travel and work together, and speak each other's language, without a hitch. The missing link in the European construction is politics. The democratic public sphere is not very noticeable. The European Parliament does brilliantly – except at election time.

The story of the Lisbon treaty is very instructive. Drafted with great care by Europe's political elite, supported strongly by business, watched with sympathy by the outside world, massively backed by national parliaments, it should at last be possible to persuade the Irish citizen to accept it in a second referendum. But this moment is decisive. If Lisbon fails again at the hands of the Irish, it will be the end of the effort to act by consensus. The pressure to break the Union up into inner and outer circles will grow. And it will surely no longer be possible to insist on the habit of rigid unanimity in order to change the Union's system of governance.

Here, as in other constitutional matters, the American founding fathers were wise. The original constitution of 1777 was a confederal arrangement where nothing could be done without the consent of all states. Only ten years later, and following the Philadelphia Convention, James Madison insisted that the new, more federal constitution should enter into force as soon as nine of the thirteen states had ratified it. It was also agreed, first, that ratification should be by way of special conventions of citizens and not simply left to the state legislative assemblies and, second, that the constitution had to be accepted or rejected in its entirety. Tactically, there was a careful sequencing of ratifications, with the five more federalist states going first, followed by four of the less zealous but still positive states. The most difficult states, New York and Virginia, undertook their ratification in the knowledge that the federal settlement had already been arrived at by others. North Carolina and Rhode Island had to vote twice to come on board, the latter two years late.

In another interesting twist, the founding fathers of the United States admitted from the outset that the constitution as drafted was not the final word. Far from over-selling the text as the ultimate settlement, as some Europeans have done with Lisbon, the Americans were bold enough to admit that further amendment would be both desirable and necessary to respond to some of the points raised during the ratification process and to meet changing circumstances (in particular the external threats from the European powers and the expansion of American territory to the West). Leaving the door open to amend the US constitution worked: the famous Bill of Rights was adopted as the first amendment as early as 1791. It has subsequently been amended on seventeen occasions.

So the Treaty of Lisbon is not the last word. The system of governance of the European Union will need to adapt further to the demands of internal integration and to the relative decline of Europe in the world, as well as to its own enlargement. Both globalisation and demography means that Europe is becoming smaller (even as it grows). Europeans are losing their moral superiority and must adjust their sights in the same way that the United States must, in Henry Kissinger's telling phrase at the inauguration of President Obama, 'modify the righteousness' of American policy. But that does not mean that either Europe or America is destined for inexorable decline. Rather the opposite conclusion can be drawn. What will save the West is the hard-headed renewal of our economic society and continuing political reform.

In particular, what will rescue the European Union from its present difficulties is a steely realisation by the states that they risk falling apart if they cannot bring themselves to be stronger together. Europe can decide whether it wants to be more united or more divided: it neither can nor will stay as it is. The challenge is to manage this federalisation process with similar skill and boldness equal to that evinced in their time by Messrs Madison, Hamilton and Jefferson.

Here, then, is a manifesto for saving the European Union:

> 1. The Treaty of Lisbon must be ratified and implemented efficiently as soon as possible. Once the new treaty is in force the Union will have acquired a unique capacity to act on the

world stage. It will be a much more powerful, open and democratic Union.

2. The EU must move quickly to establish strict, transparent supervision of the banking, securities and insurance sectors, leading to the creation of a financial services authority at the federal level. The current weak coordination of national policies should be replaced by a common macro-economic policy. A eurozone bond should be launched to restore cohesion and bolster the economic recovery plan.

3. The weak economy is no excuse to return to national protectionism. The EU should dedicate itself instead to the completion of the single market in finance, services, energy and intellectual property. Structural reforms of the labour market are badly needed to create the right conditions for renewed long-term investment. The WTO negotiations must be re-started.

4. The EU needs a radical review of its financial system. Spending should be shifted from the national to the European level to get real added value out of the Union. More spent jointly at the European level means less wasted by disjointed national efforts. The EU budget should have adequate resources, financed by fiscal federalism, to fund common policies which enhance competitiveness and create green jobs across Europe. EU spending should be made fully accountable.

5. The eurozone states must assert their autonomy from those who cannot or choose not to join the single currency. The eurogroup must act as one in world monetary matters and take the lead over the reform of the international monetary system. The Commission and the ECB

should advocate the establishment of a global network of prudential supervision across currency zones, with the longer term intention to create a world currency unit.

6. The EU must be the driving force at the UN sponsored talks on climate change. The goal is to leave Copenhagen in December 2009 with an internationally agreed package based on the EU model of cutting carbon emissions, conserving energy and increasing the use of renewables.

7. The single market must be extended to energy so that consumers benefit from a more competitive and better interconnected industry. The EU should invest directly in diversified sources of energy supply. It must help energy companies build the European super-grid as well as the infrastructure necessary to import supplies from Asia and Africa.

8. Whatever the fate of Lisbon, the EU needs to strengthen its contribution to world peace and disarmament. This means a dedicated effort to reform the United Nations as well as building up Europe's own civilian and military capability to be a credible peace-maker wherever it is needed.

9. Those EU states with the political will and the military means to do so must form a core group in security and defence. This will help NATO modernise and put transatlantic relations on a sound footing. If the Irish again reject Lisbon, the next urgent step must be to agree a separate EU treaty in security and defence between the politically willing and militarily capable EU states, excluding the rest.

10. The Union should confirm its existing commitments to enlargement, projecting its values, stability and relative prosperity

throughout its own neighbourhood. As a top priority reconciliation must be achieved between the two communities in Cyprus, united in a new federal republic.

11. The task of building Europe's common area of freedom, security and justice has only just begun. The EU urgently needs to sort out its visa policy, and fashion common policies for asylum and for legal and illegal immigration. European states must act together to combat international crime and to ensure that there is decent justice and civil liberty for all. More integration in civil law will help families and consumers.

12. The European Parliament must exercise its new democratic powers and responsibilities with energy and skill. MEPs should reform their own electoral procedure so that, in 2014, a number of deputies are elected from a single, transnational constituency. This reform is key to making European political parties fit for purpose, connecting them directly with the citizen and giving citizens a stronger voice in how Europe is run.

INDEX

179

E

L

Labour government (British), 1, 134, 153
Lamfalussy procedure, 56, 131, 136
Lamy, Pascal, 147
language, 11-12, 25, 91, 102, 124, 173
Larosière, Jacques de, 131, 136
Latvia, 135, 143
law and order, 13, 101
Law of Treaties, 111
law, EU, 14-16, 18-21, 26, 31-32, 35, 38, 55, 60-61, 68, 70, 72, 95, 97, 99-100, 117, 120, 123-124, 127, 158, 164, 168
law, international, 8, 13, 16, 20, 92, 95, 158, 168
law, national, 15, 18, 33, 35-36, 51, 56, 123, 127
Lehman Brothers, 133
Lenihan, Brian, 134, 150
Liberal Democrat and Reform party, European (ELDR), 23
Libertas, 146
liberty, 4, 18, 177
Lisbon agenda, 129, 137
Lisbon Intergovernmental Conference, 69, 108-109, 114
Lisbon, Treaty of, 6-7, 9-11, 13-16, 20, 22-26, 33, 37-38, 40-42, 45-46, 48-50, 54, 56-57, 59-65, 67, 69, 71, 73, 75, 81-83, 85, 87-88, 90, 93, 95-97, 98, 100-104, 106-109, 111-117, 121, 123, 125, 128-131, 136-146, 148-151, 153-159, 161-174, 176
loans, 66, 135
London, 37, 87, 137, 166, 170
Luxembourg, 15, 21, 106, 132

M

Maastricht, Treaty of, 7-8, 10, 17, 21-22, 50, 95, 107, 114, 135, 145, 163, 168
macroeconomic policy, 128
Madison, James, 173-174
Madriaga, Salvador de, 1
Mandelson, Peter, 143, 147
McCreevy, Charles, 142
medicine, 123
Mediterranean, 88
Message to Europeans, 2
Middle East, 5, 93
Millward Brown IMS, 149
Mitterrand, François, 1, 172
monetary union, 12, 113, 117, 129, 131, 136
multi-speed Europe, 103-104
multi-tier Europe, 104
Mussolini, 155

N

National Declaration, Irish, 168
national law, 15, 18, 33, 35-36, 51, 56, 123, 127
national parliaments, 15, 21-23, 37, 52, 55, 63, 67-72, 74, 78, 82, 85, 96, 98, 100, 109, 112-113, 115, 118, 120, 122, 141, 144, 157, 164, 173
nationalists, 70, 144, 154, 156-157, 170
NATO, 84-85, 86, 107, 139, 147-148, 176
Nazi, 171
Netherlands, 1, 9, 68, 113, 116, 141, 145, 171-172
neutrality, 83, 139, 140, 144, 162, 167
New York, 173
Nice, Treaty of, 8, 10, 18, 33, 38, 49-50, 55, 59, 63-64, 99, 101, 104, 121, 140, 144-147, 151, 153, 158-159, 166, 168-170

S

T

Lightning Source UK Ltd.
Milton Keynes UK
26 January 2010
149142UK00001B/47/P

9 781907 149023